1

MW01690838

FLORIDA

Science

McGraw Hill

FRONT COVER: Michele Oenbrink/Alamy Stock Photo
BACK COVER: Cavan Images/Cavan/Getty Images

mheducation.com/prek-12

McGraw Hill

Send all inquiries to:
McGraw Hill
8787 Orion Place
Columbus, OH 43240

ISBN: 978-1-264-91273-5
MHID: 1-264-91273-0

Printed in the United States of America.

4 5 6 7 8 9 10 11 LWI 29 28 27 26 25

Contributors

Authors

Douglas Fisher, Ph.D.
Department Chair & Professor
of Educational Leadership
San Diego State University

Jay K. Hackett, Ph.D.
Professor Emeritus of
Earth Sciences
University of Northern Colorado

Julie K. Jackson, Ph.D.
Associate Professor, Science Education
Texas State University

Page Keeley, M.Ed.
Science Consultant
Science Program Director (Retired)
Maine Mathematics and
Science Alliance

Felicia Moore Mensah, Ph.D.
Department Chair, Mathematics,
Science and Technology
Professor of Science Education
Teachers College, Columbia University

Jo Anne Vasquez, Ph.D.
Past President, National Science
Teachers Association
Rocks and Rainbows STEM and
Science Professional Learning

Dinah Zike, M.Ed.
Educational Consultant,
Inventor and Author
Dinah Zike Academy, Dinah.com

Richard Moyer, Ph.D.
In Memoriam
Professor Emeritus of Science Education and Natural Sciences
University of Michigan-Dearborn

Advisors & Consultants

Allison Antink-Meyer, Ph.D.
Professor of K-12 Science and
Engineering Education
Illinois State University

Texas A&M University
Center for Research & Development
in Dual Language & Literacy Acquisition

Rafael Lara-Alecio, Ph.D.
Director of CRDLLA
Regents Professor
Texas A&M University

Dr. Beverly J. Irby
Co-Director of CRDLLA
Regents Professor
Texas A&M University

Fuhui Tong, Ph.D.
Professor
Texas A&M University

Dr. Cindy Guerrero
CRDLLA Research Scientist
Texas A&M University

Teacher Reviewers & Advisory Board

Fredesvinda Monique Andrews, M.S.
Elementary Education Grades K–6
Miami-Dade County Public Schools
Miami, Florida

Kathleen Cattie
Miami-Dade County Public Schools
Miami, Florida

Nicole E. Curtiss, M.Ed.
K–8 Math and Science Education
Orange County Public Schools
Orlando, Florida

Isabel Lopez Garcia
Miami-Dade County Public Schools
Miami, Florida

Suzanne Mason, M.Ed.
Elementary Science Coach
Hillsborough County Public Schools
Tampa, Florida

Anji McStravic
Elementary Science Coach
Lee County School District
Fort Myers, Florida

Yanell Sanchez, M.Ed.
Miami-Dade County Public Schools
Miami, Florida

Tameika Scott Smith, M.Ed.
Elementary Science/Math Coach
Orange County Public Schools
Orlando, Florida

CHAPTER 1 FSAS SC.1.N.1.1, SC.1.N.1.2, SC.1.N.1.3, SC.1.N.1.4

Onward We Go

How do inventions help people?

GO ONLINE **Digital Spotlight**

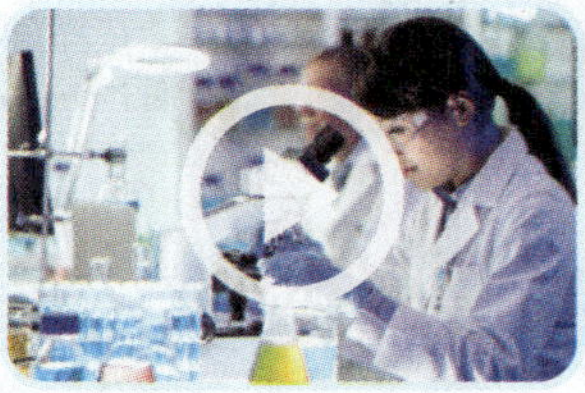

Chapter Launch Video
How Do Inventions Help People?

STEM Connection Video
Meet an Electrical Engineer

Interactive Infographic
The Problem of the Rolling Pencil

CHAPTER 2 FSAS SC.1.E.5.1, SC.1.E.5.2, SC.1.E.5.3, SC.1.E.5.4

Earth and Space

What can you see from Earth?

GO ONLINE **Digital Spotlight**

Chapter Launch Video
What Can You See from Earth?

Interactive Infographic
The Effects of Gravity

STEM Connection
Draw Her Life with Dana Bolles

CHAPTER 3 FSAS SC.1.E.6.1, SC.1.E.6.2, SC.1.E.6.3

Earth's Surface

What's around the bend?

GO ONLINE **Digital Spotlight**

Chapter Launch Video
What's Around the Bend?

EXPLAIN It Video
Plants and Animals Use Earth Materials

Observe Your World Video
Eruption!

STEM PROJECT Earth Materials in Everyday Life

CHAPTER 4 FSAS SC.1.L.14.1, SC.1.L.14.2, SC.1.L.14.3, SC.1.L.17.1

Living and Nonliving Things are Connected

Do turtles need plants?

GO ONLINE **Digital Spotlight**

Chapter Launch Video
Do Turtles Need Plants?

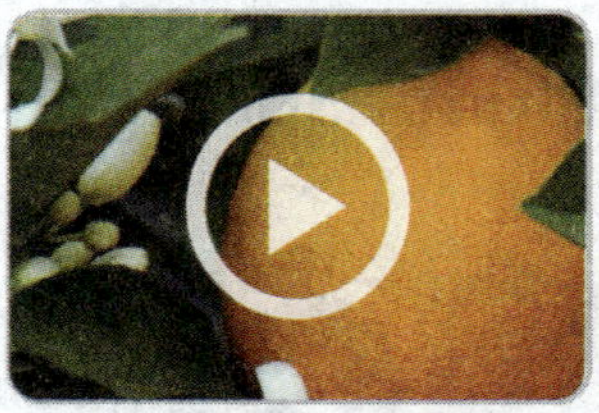

EXPLAIN It Video
Parts of a Plant

STEM Connection Video
Jenny Adler's Profile

STEM PROJECT Terrific Terrariums

CHAPTER 5 FSAS SC.1.L.14.1, SC.1.L.16.1

Plant and Animal Observations

How are these living things alike?

GO ONLINE **Digital Spotlight**

Chapter Launch Video
How are These Living Things Alike?

EXPLAIN It Video
Animal Families

STEM Connection Video
GrowNYC

CHAPTER 6 FSAS SC.1.P.8.1

Sorting Matter

How are toys unique?

GO ONLINE **Digital Spotlight**

Chapter Launch Video
How are Toys Unique?

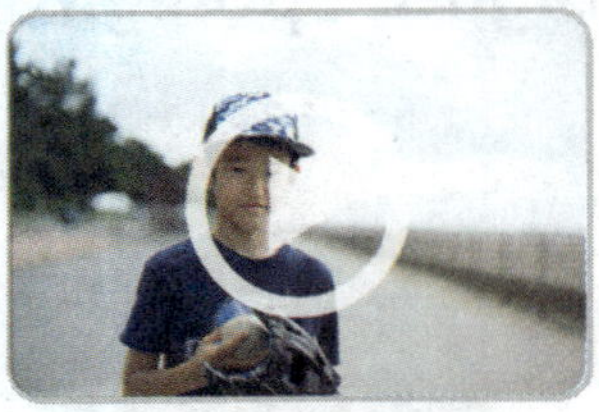

EXPLAIN It Video
Classifying Objects

STEM Connection Video
Camp GoldieBlox: Karina Popovich

STEM PROJECT Family Night Scavenger Hunt

CHAPTER 7 FSAS SC.1.P.12.1, SC.1.P.13.1

Forces and Motion

What's happening at the water park?

GO ONLINE **Digital Spotlight**

Chapter Launch Video
What's Happening at the Water Park?

Interactive Infographic
Learn About Investigations

STEM Connection Video
Meet an Engineer and an Astronaut

STEM PROJECT Fun with Forces

CHAPTER 1

Onward We Go

Check it out!

How do inventions help people?

SC.1.N.1.1 Raise questions about the natural world, investigate them in teams through free exploration, and generate appropriate explanations based on those explorations.

SC.1.N.1.2 Using the five senses as tools, make careful observations, describe objects in terms of number, shape, texture, size, weight, color, and motion, and compare their observations with others.

SC.1.N.1.3 Keep records as appropriate - such as pictorial and written records - of investigations conducted.

SC.1.N.1.4 Ask “how do you know?” in appropriate situations.

Meet an Electrical Engineer

Guillermo González Camarena was an electrical engineer. He came up with a way for cameras to take pictures in color. He then discovered how to send them. This is why televisions have color pictures. Before that, they could only show pictures in black and white.

Can you imagine watching your favorite cartoon with no color? Thanks to Guillermo González Camarena, you can watch your favorite shows in color. His invention also helped children learn. They could learn by watching shows that taught them things!

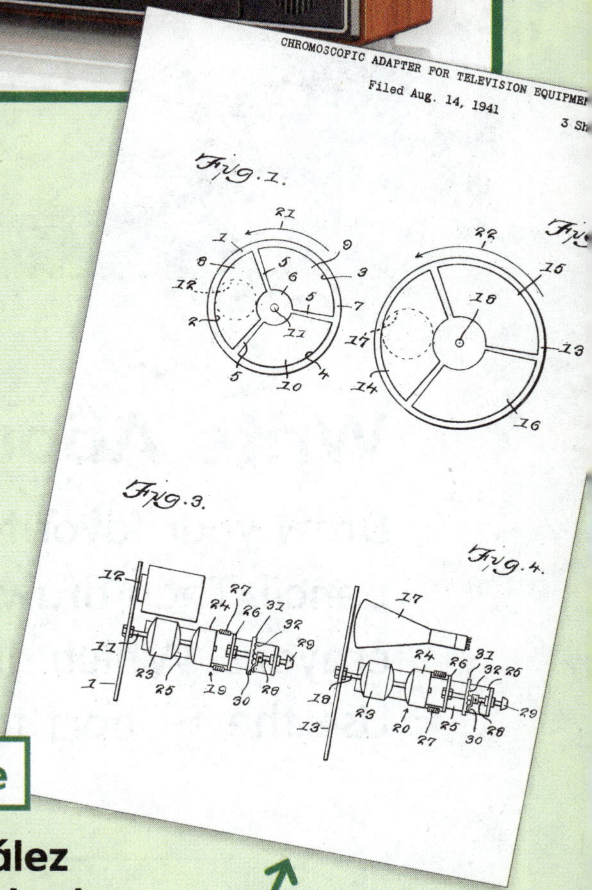

Primary Source

Guillermo González Camarena sketched his design.

Watch *Meet an Electrical Engineer.*

Write About It!

Draw your favorite cartoon character using a pencil. Then draw the same character with crayons. Which drawing do you like more? Use the T-Chart to organize your information.

T-Chart

Write About It! Which drawing do you find more interesting? Write a short response explaining why. ELA.K12.EE.5.1

Claim, Evidence, Reasoning

Step 1

Write a claim.
A claim is what you think is true.

I claim that ________.

Step 2

Gather evidence.
Evidence is what you observe.

I think ________
because ________.

Step 3

Write reasoning.
Reasoning is why you think something is true.

My claim is valid
because ________.

Descriptive Investigations

Think about something you would like to know. Do you know you can follow steps to find the answer?

Science is using evidence to explain and predict phenomena.

A **scientist** is a person who uses evidence to explain. Scientists conduct investigations.

You can do investigations, too. All investigations start with a question.

How would a descriptive investigation help someone trying to invent something?

Talk About It Why would a scientist investigate popcorn?

Scientists conduct **descriptive investigations** to answer a question and make a claim. They follow steps.

How are these pieces being picked up?

Science Skills

Ask: What is the question?

Plan: Write steps to answer the question.

Conduct: Follow the steps.

Record: Describe what you observe.

Communicate: Explain what you found out.

Record what you observe.

Hands-On Investigation

Magnet Investigation

SC.1.N.1.1 SC.1.N.1.3

Get your notebook and go explore!

Tools and Safety

Scientists use tools. They use tools to observe things. They use tools to **measure** things. They use tools to test things.

safety goggles

Scientists use tools to stay safe. They use safety tools when performing descriptive investigations.

Sometimes scientists investigate outside. They are called field investigations. They use safe practices outside too.

heat-resistant gloves

DIRECTIONS Identify and describe the safe practices the student in the photo is using during their investigation.

Talk About It Identify and describe ways to stay safe when doing field investigations.

Build Your Skill

Being Safe

1. It is time to take something off the hot plate.
2. You need a tool that will cover your hands.
3. You need a tool that will cover your wrists.
4. You need a tool that will protect your skin from the heat.

Tools and Criteria

	cover hands	cover wrists	protect skin from heat
 tray	☐	☐	☐
 tweezers	☐	☐	☐
 heat-resistant gloves	☐	☐	☐

DIRECTIONS Apply It 1. Observe the tools in the table. 2. Complete the table. Record the criteria each tool meets by checking the correct boxes. 3. Which tool meets all three of the required criteria? SC.1.N.1.3
Write About It! What other problem can you solve using one of these tools? Draw and label a picture. ELA.K12.EE.1.1

Engineering Design Process

Engineers identify problems. They design solutions.

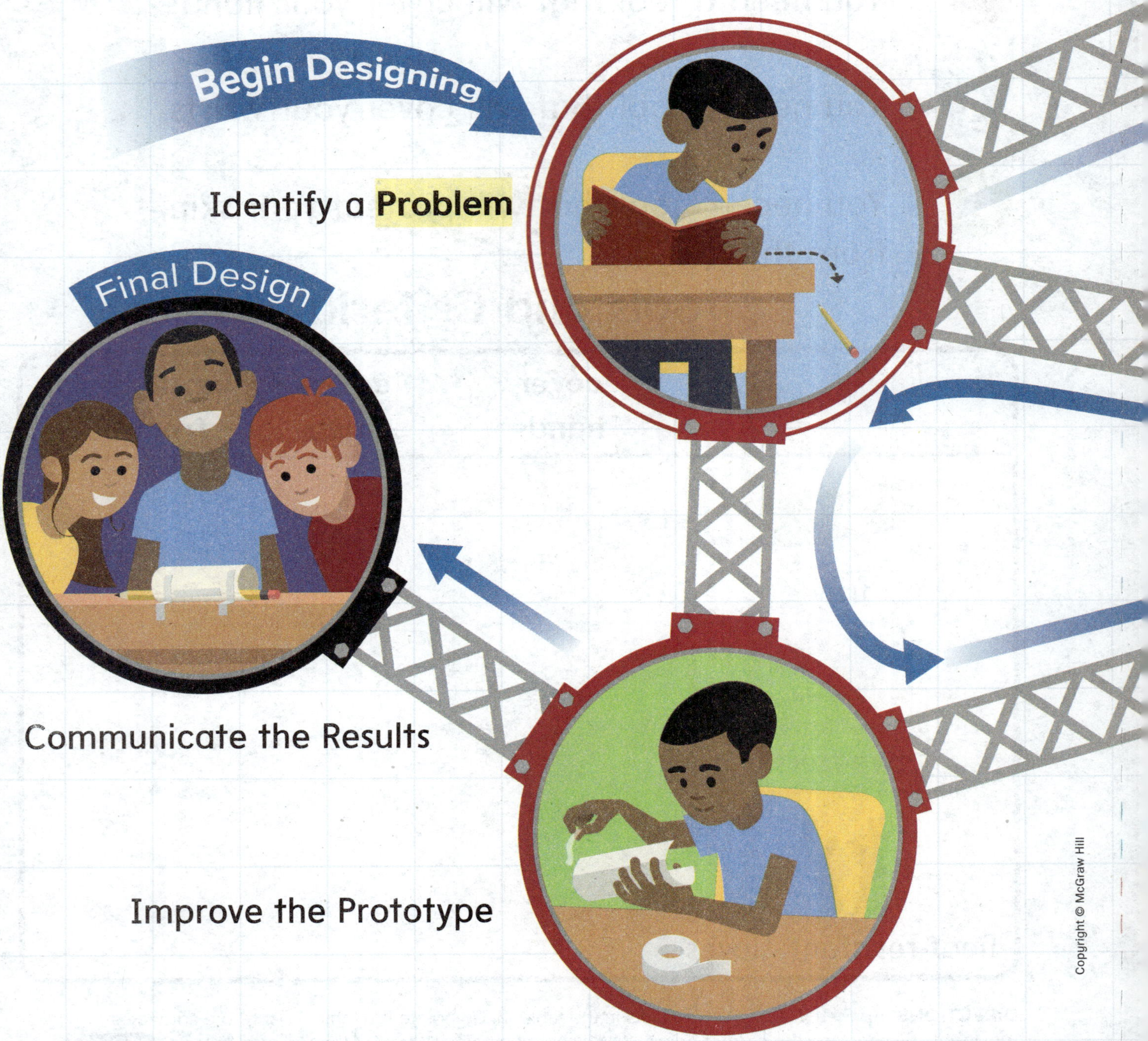

DIRECTIONS Read the Infographic Evaluate the two designs on the infographic. Do they work as intended? Using data from the infographic, propose your own solution to this problem.

Talk About It Identify an engineer you have learned about.

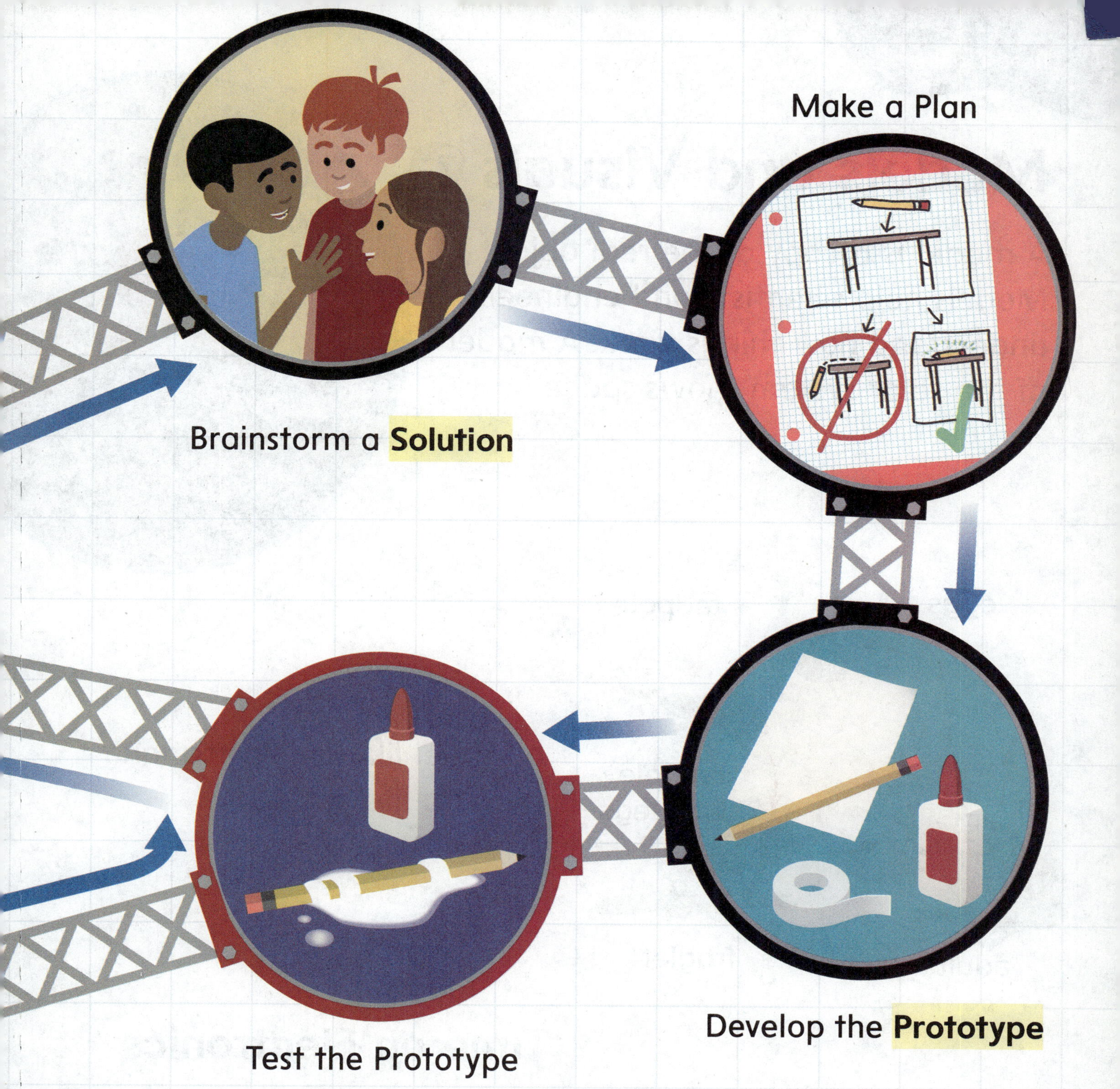

Hands-On Investigation

Track Time

SC.1.N.1.1 SC.1.N.1.3

Get your notebook and go explore!

Read Together

Models and Visuals

A model is a copy of the real object. Models help scientists and engineers understand how things work. A model of the solar system shows space.

A model like an illustration shows a life cycle.

A model like a bar graph shows data.

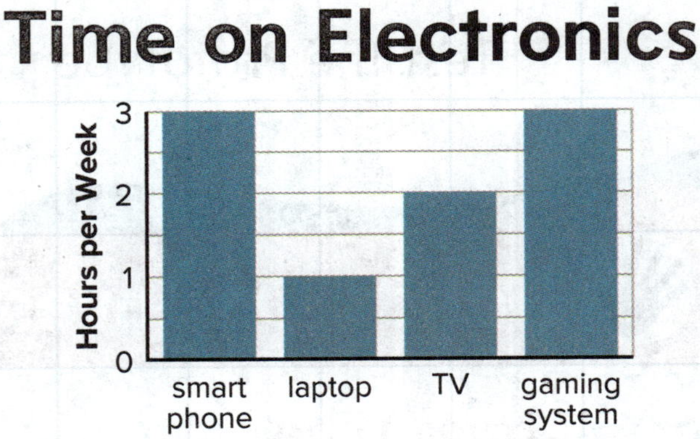

What are other inventions that scientists use?

Talk About It Look at the bar graph. What questions do you have? How many hours do you spend on technology?

See, Scan, Analyze

A model is an example of a visual. Using visuals can help us learn about a topic. You will use visuals to learn science.

Observe the visual.

See: What is this?

Scan: What is the visual trying to show me?

Analyze: What information can I gather?

DIRECTIONS Read the Photo 1. What is the photo showing? 2. What are different ways this invention can help you? 3. Are there other inventions like this one?

Data Literacy

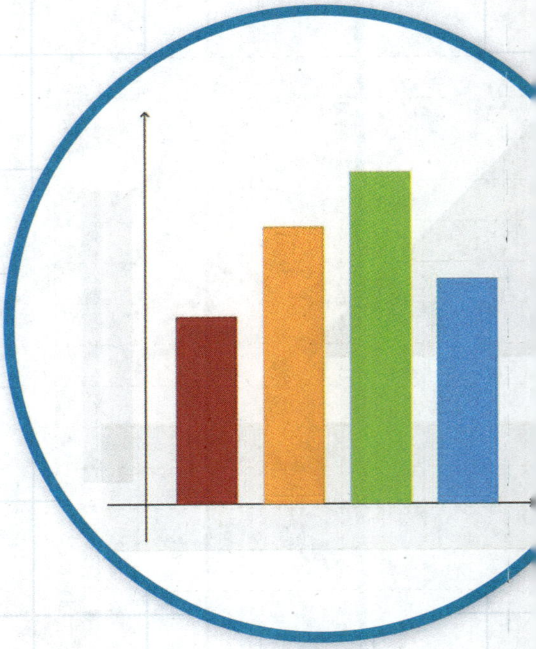

Scientists and engineers use data. Data shows facts and information. Data can be pictures. Data can be words. Data can be numbers. Graphs show data.

Graphs can show how data is related. They can show measurements. They can show patterns in data. They can show significant features.

There are different kinds of graphs. Some are called bar graphs. Some are called picture graphs.

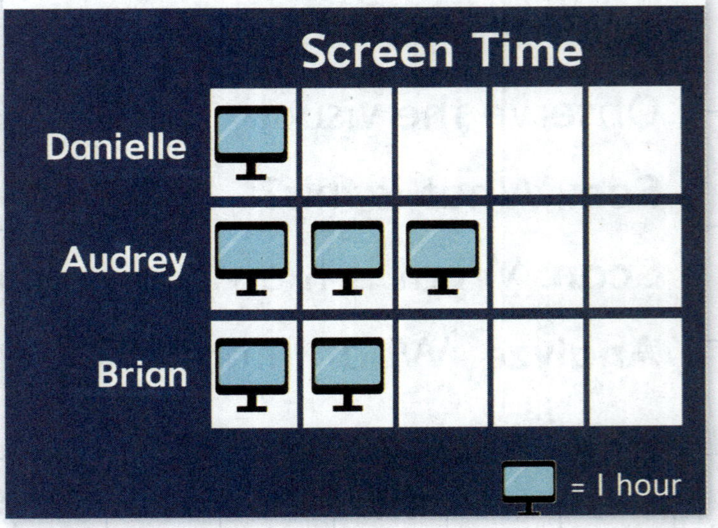

DIRECTIONS **Read the Graph** Look at the Screen Time picture graph. Count and record in your notebook the number of hours in each row. Plan a descriptive investigation to explore the screen time in your classroom during the school day.

Build Your Skill

Boat Builder

Randy enters a boat race. He designs this model boat. What problems might Randy's boat have?

DIRECTIONS Apply It 1. What materials do you think will work better for the model? 2. How do you know? SC.1.N.1.4
Write About It! Help Randy design a prototype of a boat that will make it across the river. ELA.K12.EE.3.1

Research and Communication

Scientific information is not just important to scientists and engineers. It helps everyone.

Scientists and engineers learn from each other. They do research. Then they read each other's results. They ask questions and define problems based on phenomena.

Scientists and engineers communicate. They talk, write, and draw. They also listen to ideas and treat each other with respect.

Talk About It Why is it important for scientists and engineers to work together?

Science Thinking Tools

Patterns

What patterns do you see?
How does the pattern repeat?

Cause and Effect

What causes things to happen?
What are the effects?

Scale, Proportion, and Quantity

How big is it?
How many are there?

Systems and System Models

What are the parts?
How do the parts work together?

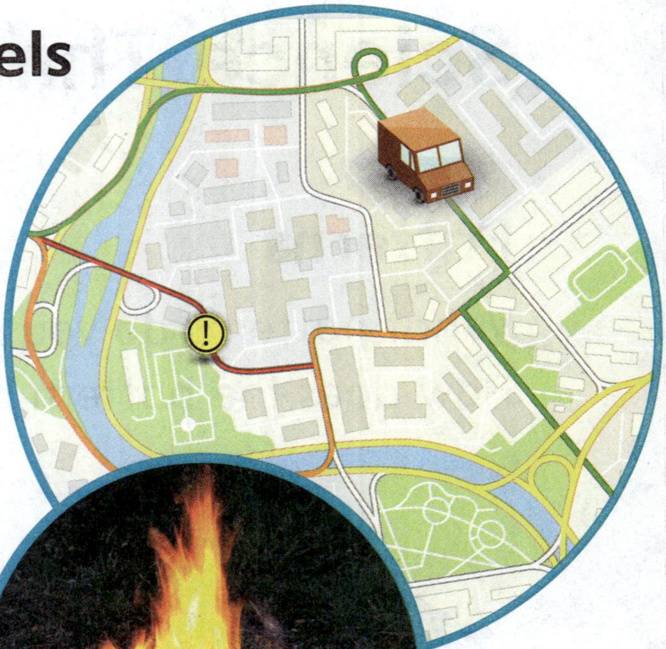

Energy and Matter

What causes things to change?
What is an object made of?

Structure and Function

What structures do you see?
What do the structures do?

Stability and Change

How do things change?
How do they stay the same?

Am I Ready?

Draw and label a picture of technology you use.

How do inventions help people?

Color to reflect on your learning.

Chapter Review

1

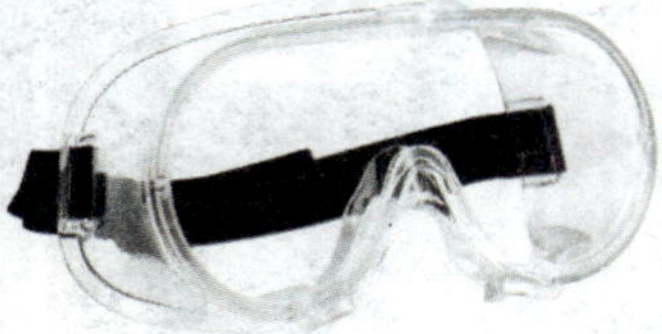

2

- guesses how things work
- uses evidence to explain

3

- They are not important.
- They help people.
- They help no one.

DIRECTIONS 1. Circle the safety tool that scientists and engineers use. 2. What does a scientist do? Check the box. 3. Why are inventions important? Check the box. SC.1.N.1.2

CHAPTER 2
Earth and Space

Check it out!

What can you see from Earth?

SC.1.E.5.1 Observe and discuss that there are more stars in the sky than anyone can easily count and that they are not scattered evenly in the sky.

SC.1.E.5.2 Explore the Law of Gravity by demonstrating that Earth's gravity pulls any object on or near Earth toward it even though nothing is touching the object.

SC.1.E.5.3 Investigate how magnifiers make things appear bigger and help people see things they could not see without them.

SC.1.E.5.4 Identify the beneficial and harmful properties of the Sun.

Chapter Preview

Take Note!

DIRECTIONS What did you see in the video that interested you? Draw a picture.

PAGE KEELEY SCIENCE PROBES

Stars in the Sky

Elmer

I think we see stars only in the daytime.

Lucy

I think we see stars only in the nighttime.

I think we see stars in the daytime and in the nighttime.

Anna

DIRECTIONS Circle who you agree with.
Talk About It Who did you circle? Why? Show a partner.

Essential Question

How can you see things that are hard to see?

Watch *Massive Moon.*

Hands-On Investigation

Moon Over the Night Sky

SC.1.N.1.2 SC.1.N.1.3

Get your notebook and go explore!

Stars Above

Have you ever looked up at the night sky? You might have seen clouds, the Moon, and **stars**. Stars are objects in the sky that make their own light.

Stars look tiny because they are far away. There are more stars than anyone can easily count. Stars are not scattered evenly in the sky.

Stars can form patterns in the sky. Some patterns might look like people, animals, or objects.

DIRECTIONS Think about the Moon Over the Night Sky investigation. Now, read to learn more.

The Sun is a star. It is the closest star to Earth.

Sunlight is so bright that you cannot see other stars during the day.

At night, after the Sun sets, we are able to see other stars.

Investigation Connection Think about a time when you looked at the night sky. Did you see more than stars?

Talk About It Share your answers with a partner.

A Closer Look

Magnifiers

People use tools to see more clearly. Some tools **magnify** objects. Binoculars help us see things that are far away.

binoculars

telescope

A telescope makes far-away objects look larger and closer. Telescopes help us see things that we could not see without them.

The magnified photo shows stars through a telescope. How are the stars different in the photo that is not magnified?

What could a microscope help you see on Earth?

Quick Lab Get ready to explore. SC.1.N.1.3

Other tools help people see tiny details. A microscope makes small objects look big. Microscopes help us see things that we could not see without them.

A hand lens magnifies small objects too. Hand lenses help us see small things clearly.

Magnified Match	

DIRECTIONS Look at the Magnified Match pictures with a partner. The objects are magnified, or shown up close. Talk about the objects and what they could be.

Observe Your World

John Glenn Astronomy Park

Look up to the Sky

A stargazer looks at the night sky. You can be a stargazer too.

This park has 12 telescopes.
They magnify objects in the night sky.

The objects appear bigger and are easier to see.
You can see more stars when the sky is clear.

Write About It! Think about ways you can look at the night sky. Record your thoughts in your notebook. Use words from the Interactive Word Wall ELA.K12.EE.1.1

Am I Ready?

What is one tool that makes things appear bigger? Draw a picture of yourself using that tool.

Describe an object you could look at using the tool you drew.

Color to reflect on your learning.

Lesson Review

1

2

- [ ] smaller
- [ ] bigger

3

- [ ] evenly
- [ ] unevenly

DIRECTIONS 1. Circle the photos that show what you would see with a hand lens 2. How will objects appear when you look through a telescope? Check the box. 3. Are stars scattered evenly or unevenly in the night sky? Check the box. SC.1.E.5.1 SC.1.E.5.3

PAGE KEELEY SCIENCE PROBES

Objects and Gravity

drums

girl

boat

lamp

tree

rabbit

bird

waterfall

rock

DIRECTIONS Circle the objects affected by gravity.
Talk About It What did you circle? Why? Show a partner.

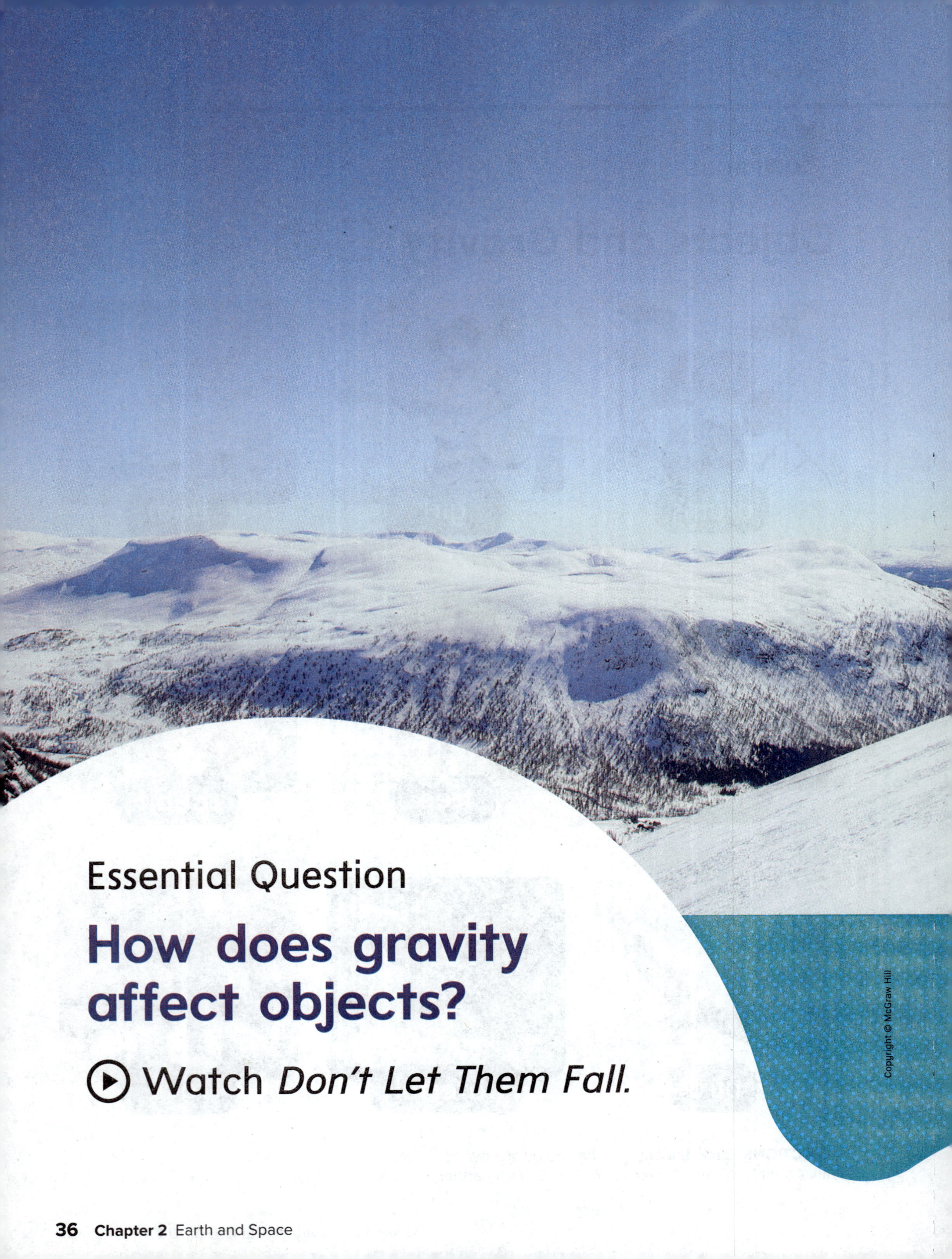

Essential Question

How does gravity affect objects?

Watch *Don't Let Them Fall.*

Hands-On Investigation

The Force of Gravity

SC.1.N.1.1 SC.1.N.1.3

Get your notebook and go explore!

Gravity and You

After you jump, you come back down. **Gravity** is a force that pulls everything back to Earth.

Gravity pulls on objects even if nothing is touching them. When an egg is dropped, gravity pulls it down.

You cannot see gravity, but it is always there. When you toss an object into the air, gravity pulls it back down.

DIRECTIONS Think about The Force of Gravity investigation. Now, read to learn more.

Gravity pulls this skydiver to Earth. The parachute keeps them safe.

Jumping rope would be very different without gravity! Gravity pulls the child and the rope back to the ground.

Gravity pulls on all objects. Gravity pulls the dolphins back down. Gravity pulls this athlete back down, too.

Can you see gravity on Earth?

Investigation Connection How could you improve your investigation to show other examples of gravity?

Where is Gravity?

Observe the day at the park. Gravity is everywhere! How does gravity affect things on or near Earth's surface?

DIRECTIONS **Read the Infographic.** 1. What examples of gravity do you see? 2. How do the objects move? 3. Think of an example you could add to the picture.

Talk About It Discuss with a partner.

STEM Connection IF/THEN

This Is What A Scientist Looks Like®

Meet a Spaceflight Engineer

When Dana Bolles was young, she wanted to be an astronaut. She grew up without arms and legs, so she learned to use technology to help herself. Technology helps her in many ways. She has artificial arms. She uses an electric wheelchair. She drives a special van.

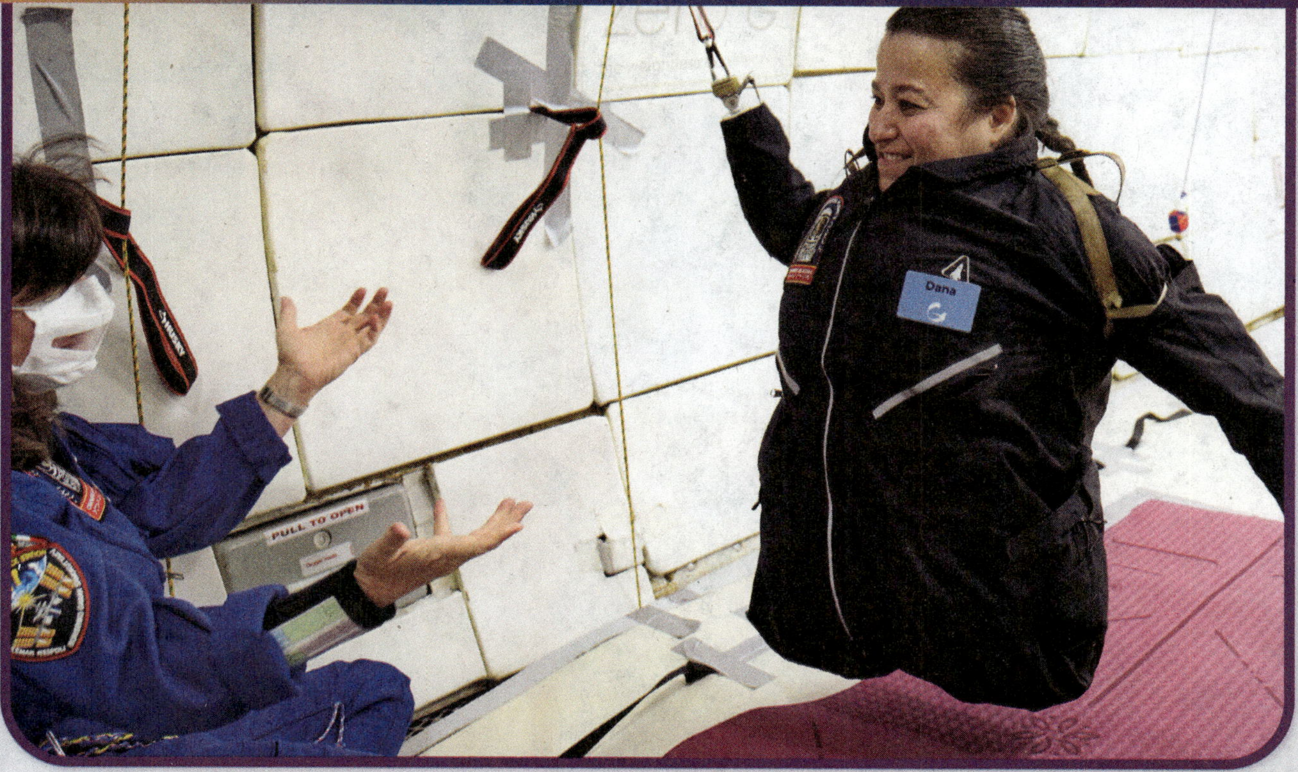

Dana Bolles wanted to learn how to fix these things. She became an engineer. She learned how to make new tools. She learned how to keep her equipment working well. She became a spaceflight engineer. She felt zero gravity on a plane. She floated! She said it felt incredible. Now, she looks for life beyond Earth. She looks for Goldilocks planets. These planets are in places that are not too hot and not too cold.

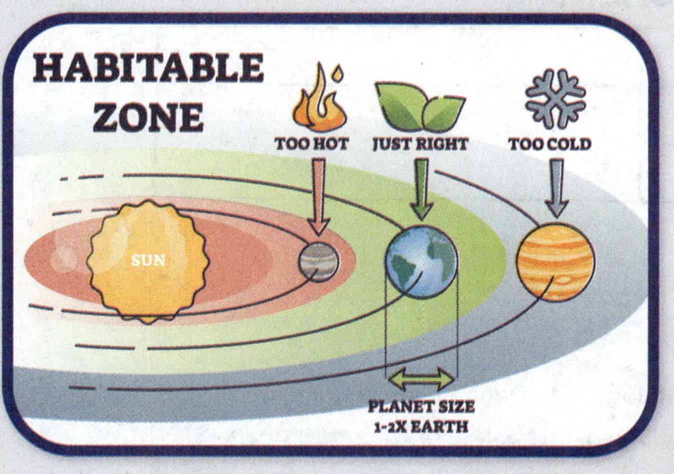

Watch *Draw Her Life with Dana Bolles.*

Dana Bolles tells students to keep positive people around you. They will support you and your goals.

Write About It!

How does technology help Dana Bolles do things? Organize your information.

T-Chart

Write About It! Observe the photos. How does technology help Dana Bolles do things? Draw a picture. Use words from the Interactive Word Wall to label your picture. ELA.K12.EE.1.1

Am I Ready?

Draw an object that is affected by gravity.

Describe where gravity pulls the object.

Color to reflect on your learning.

Lesson Review

1

2

- [ ] yes
- [ ] no

3

- [ ] The water goes up.
- [ ] The water goes down.
- [ ] The water is loud.

DIRECTIONS 1. Which photos have things that are affected by gravity? Circle the photos. 2. Does something have to be touching an object for gravity to affect it? Check the box with the correct answer. 3. How does gravity affect the water in the waterfall? Check the box. SC.1.E.5.2

PAGE KEELEY SCIENCE PROBES

Warm Sand

Ellie

The wind warms the sand.

Sita

The Sun warms the sand.

The water warms the sand.

Ren

DIRECTIONS Who do you think has the better idea? Circle their photo.
Talk About It What did you circle? Why? Show a partner.

Essential Question

When is the Sun helpful and harmful?

Watch *So Much Sunshine.*

Lesson 3

Miami, FL

Hands-On Investigation

Changes from the Sun

SC.1.N.1.1 SC.1.N.1.3

Get your notebook and go explore!

The Sun and Earth

How does the Sun affect Earth's surface? We need the Sun because it gives us light and heat.

Heat from the Sun keeps Earth at a temperature that is good for living and growing things.

You can feel the Sun's heat when sunlight shines on you.

DIRECTIONS Think about the Changes from the Sun investigation. Now, read to learn more.

The Sun's energy warms the air, land, and water. All living things depend on the Sun.

Without the Sun, it would be too cold for us to live and grow things on Earth.

During the day, the Sun lights up the Earth. Without light, it would be hard to see things outside.

Investigation Connection What other objects could you add to your investigation?
Talk About It Share your answers with a partner.

Sunlight

On some days, sunlight makes the air feel hot. Air that is too hot can be **harmful**.

Getting too hot can hurt the ground, plants, and animals. People can become sick, too.

Sunscreen and sunglasses will protect you from the Sun. Drink water to keep your body hydrated. How do you cool off on a hot day?

The Sun is **beneficial** in many ways. Lots of sunlight helps plants grow. Plants are food for people and animals. The Sun helps farmers and gardeners grow crops.

Sometimes it is not too hot or too cold. It feels good to be outside in the sunshine.

How do you spend time outside?

What does sunlight help you see on Earth?

Observe Your World

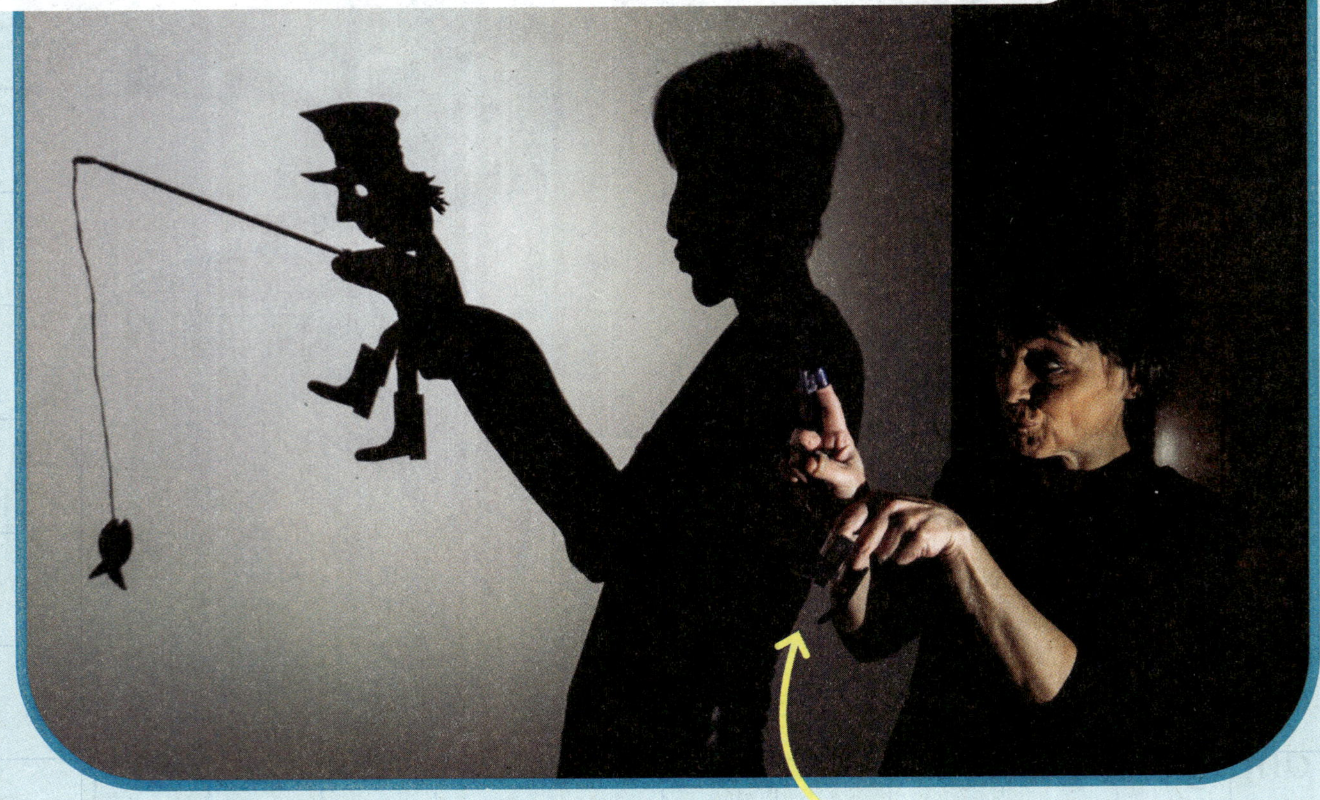

People use their hands to make shadow puppets.

Shadow Puppets

You need light to see shadows. The Sun, lamps, and even campfires are light sources. Shadows can be made with just your hands and light. Moving shadows, like these shadow puppets, can even tell a story.

What kinds of shadows would these fish make?

Write About It! Draw and label a picture of a shadow puppet show in your notebook. Draw a light source you could use.

Use words from the Interactive Word Wall ELA.K12.EE.5.1

Am I Ready?

Draw a picture showing how the Sun can be helpful.

What is one way the Sun can be harmful?

Color to reflect on your learning.

Lesson Review

1

2

3

- [ ] The Sun's light helps people see outside.
- [ ] The Sun's energy warms the Earth.
- [ ] The Sun's energy cools the Earth.

DIRECTIONS 1. How can you protect yourself when you are outside in the Sun? Circle the photos. 2. Circle the photo that shows a harmful effect of the Sun. 3. How is the Sun helpful? Check all the boxes that fit. SC.1.E.5.4

CHAPTER 3

Earth's Surface

Check it out!

What's around the bend?

SC.1.E.6.1 Recognize that water, rocks, soil, and living organisms are found on Earth's surface.

SC.1.E.6.2 Describe the need for water and how to be safe around water.

SC.1.E.6.3 Recognize that some things in the world around us happen fast and some happen slowly.

Chapter Preview

Let's learn!

Take Note!

DIRECTIONS What did you see in the video that interested you? Draw a picture.

PAGE KEELEY SCIENCE PROBES

Things Found on Earth's Surface

sand

ice

snow

rocks

soil

animals

people

water

plants

DIRECTIONS Circle the objects that are part of Earth's surface.
Talk About It What objects did you circle? Why? Show a partner.

Essential Question

What can be found on Earth's surface?

Watch *On the Surface.*

Hands-On Investigation

Describing Earth

SC.1.N.1.3

Get your notebook and go explore!

Describe Earth's Surface

Think about your last walk outside. What did you see? Earth's surface is covered with interesting things.

Rocks are hard, nonliving parts of Earth. Some are shiny. Others are dull.

Rocks have different shapes, sizes, and colors.

DIRECTIONS Think about the Describing Earth investigation. Now, read to learn more.

Quick Lab Get ready to explore. SC.1.N.1.2 SC.1.N.1.3

Soil is made of many things. It is made of tiny pieces of rocks. Water and air are in soil too. Soils can have plant, animal, and mineral parts in them. Plants get nutrients from soil. A nutrient is something that living things need to grow.

Types of Soil

topsoil	Topsoil is brown. It feels crumbly. It has small and large particles.	
clay soil	Clay soil is red. It feels smooth and slippery. It has small particles.	
sandy soil	Sandy soil is tan. It feels rough. It has large particles.	

Investigation Connection Review your list from the investigation. Can you think of something else to add? Work with a partner to add something new to each of your lists.

Our Earth

Earth is made of land and water.
Water covers most of Earth.
What else is found on Earth's surface?

Talk About It Where is the water in this photo of Earth?

Does Earth's surface always look the same?

Living Organisms

You can also find living **organisms** on Earth's surface. Organisms are living things, such as plants, animals, and people. Living organisms live on rocks, in water, and in soil. You can find living things all over Earth.

Watch *Plants and Animals Use Earth Materials.*

DIRECTIONS **Read the Diagram** Observe the diagram of the forest. Circle the organisms you see.
Talk About It How are rocks, soil, and water important to the plants and animals in the diagram? Share your ideas with a partner.

Build Your Skill

Investigate Your Data

Scientists use data to solve problems. Think about different types of soils. Help Oliver choose the best one.

Apply It

Oliver needs soil for his garden.

He wants dark brown soil.
He wants soil with small and large particles in it.
He wants the soil to feel crumbly.

What kind of soil should Oliver use?

DIRECTIONS Apply It Think about the different types of soil. Which one would be the best for Oliver's new plant? SC.1.N.1.2
Write About It! Draw and label a picture of Oliver planting a flower. Add details to describe the properties of the soil he is using. ELA.K12.EE.1.1

Use words from the Interactive Word Wall to label your drawing.

Am I Ready?

Draw a picture to show something that can be found on Earth's surface.

Describe what you drew and where it is found.

Color to reflect on your learning.

Lesson Review

1

rocks

soil

- [ ] Rocks are made of small pieces of soil.
- [ ] Soil is made of small pieces of rock.

2

3

- [ ] rocks
- [ ] water
- [ ] soil

DIRECTIONS 1. Which statement about rocks and soil is correct? Check the box. 2. Circle the photo that shows living organisms. 3. Which covers most of Earth's surface? Check the box. SC.1.E.6.1

PAGE KEELEY SCIENCE PROBES

Uses for Water

washing clothes

growing food

keeping cool

taking a drink

cooking food

transporting goods

keeping clean

having fun

DIRECTIONS Where do you see ways that people use water? Circle the photos.
Talk About It What did you circle? Why? Show a partner.

Essential Question

Why do we need water?

Watch *What's up with Water?*

Hands-On Investigation

Water Survey

SC.1.N.1.3

Get your notebook and go explore!

Water, Water Everywhere!

Water is found all over Earth's surface. All living things need water. A river is a large stream of flowing water.

Suwannee River, FL

Lake Eola Park, FL

Lakes are surrounded by land. Most rivers and lakes are made of **fresh water**.

An ocean is a large, deep body of **salt water**. Oceans cover most of Earth's surface.

DIRECTIONS Think about the Water Survey investigation. Now, read to learn more.

People use water for many things. We need water to drink.

We use water to cook food, wash clothes, and water plants.

We use water and soap to keep clean. We wash our hands, brush our teeth, and clean our homes. Keeping clean helps us stay healthy.

How do living things use rivers, lakes, and oceans?

More Bodies of Water

Water can help us get items we need.
This boat floats on water.
It brings things from far away.

Water is used to make machines move.
Water turns a wheel.
The wheel turns parts of a machine.

DIRECTIONS **Read the Diagram** Observe the parts of the mill. How does the water turn gears in the mill?
Talk About It Share your answers with a partner.

Water Safety

People like to play in water. Swimming and water sports can be fun. It is important to follow safety rules when you are near water. Safety rules keep people safe.

Staying Safe Around Water

	Wear a life jacket.
	Do not dive into a lake or river. It could be shallow.
	Have an adult watch you near water. Always swim with a buddy.
	Never use electricity around water.

Watch *Bodies of Water.*

Investigation Connection Review the results of the investigation. What were the two most common ways your classmates use water?

DIRECTIONS **Read the Table** 1. Observe each photo in the table. 2. Talk to a partner about a water safety rule you could add to the table.

STEM Connection

Meet an Oceans Program Director

Katie Doyle is a teacher.
She teaches students in the Oceans Program.
They do research to study air and water.
They study wetlands, too. Katie Doyle thinks students can make a difference. They can use less plastic. They can pick up trash.
It will help the oceans on Earth.

Katie Doyle also works on the *Nautilus*. Scientists use the *Nautilus* to study the oceans. Katie Doyle works in a studio on the ship. From there, she talks to classrooms around the world. She explains what scientists are learning.

Katie Doyle shares ocean discoveries with classrooms around the world.

Watch *Meet an Oceans Program Director and Nautilus Crew Member.*

Katie Doyle gets excited about new discoveries. Then she shares them with the world!

Write About It!

Katie Doyle thinks students can make a difference! How can you use less plastic to help the oceans? Organize your information.

Topic and Details

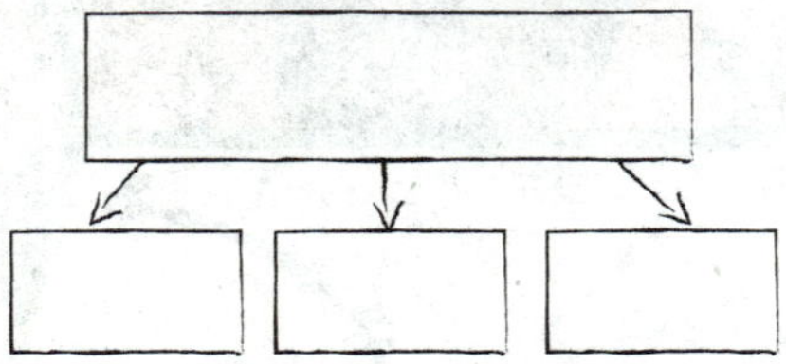

Write About It! Draw and label a picture of one way you can use less plastic.

Use words from the Interactive Word Wall to help you write a sentence and label your picture. ELA.K12.EE.5.1

Am I Ready?

Draw someone using water safely. Label your drawing.

Explain how your drawing shows someone using water safely.

because he is not using electricity. Someone is using water safely

Color to reflect on your learning.

Lesson Review

1

- fresh water
- salt water

2

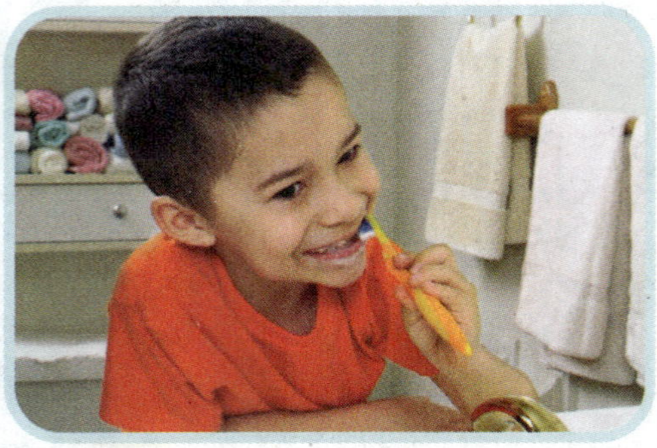

3

- to clean
- to breathe
- to drink

DIRECTIONS 1. What kind of water is the ocean made up of? Check the box. 2.Circle the photo that shows someone practicing water safety. 3. Why do people use water? Check two boxes. SC.1.E.6.2

PAGE KEELEY SCIENCE PROBES

Moving Water

DIRECTIONS Who do you agree with? Circle their picture or name.
Talk About It Who did you circle? Explain your thinking to a partner.

Essential Question

How do water and wind move rocks and soil?

Watch *Serene Stream.*

Hands-On Investigation

Go with the Flow

SC.1.N.1.1

Get your notebook and go explore!

Water Changes Earth's Surface

Earth's surface can **change**. Things can break apart and move. Sometimes changes happen **slowly**. Slow-flowing streams carry small rocks in the water. Larger rocks sink to the bottom. Because of this, slow-flowing streams make slow changes to Earth's surface.

This stream is carrying soil particles. Soil particles make the water muddy. What happens to rocks and soil that are carried by streams?

DIRECTIONS Think about the Go with the Flow investigation. Now, read to learn more.

Rocks and soil can be carried all the way to the ocean. Sometimes they are carried out to sea.

Ocean waves can move rocks, sand, and soil. Sometimes waves bring these materials onto the shore.

Investigation Connection How did flowing water change the hill? Which parts of the hill were carried by the water?

Talk About It Describe the streams in the photos. Which ones could carry a rock in its flowing water? Explain your thinking.

Wind Changes Earth's Surface

Land can change slowly. Over time, erosion happens. This happens when wind and water move rocks and soil to new places.

FL Ponte Vedra Beach, FL

Water can slowly wash away pieces of rocks and sand. The wind can pick up and move sand.

Check out *Earth Materials Move!*

Plants can help some changes from happening. A plant's roots help hold soil in place. This makes it harder for wind and water to move the soil.

People can plant grasses to help slow these changes. Change happens more slowly.

DIRECTIONS **Read the Photo** What things can water and wind change in these photos?

Can water and wind affect things differently in different places? Why?

Observe Your World

Sand can help save the Bayou!

Trouble in the Bayou

Water moves soil in the Salt Bayou. This changes the land. Some of these changes are bad for the plants and animals that live there. Experts want to help! They use large piles of sand to block the water. This helps the wildlife.

Watch *Down in the Bayou.*

Write About It! Draw and label the Salt Bayou and the sand piles that help block the water. Use words from the Interactive Word Wall to label your drawing. ELA.K12.EE.1.1

Am I Ready?

Draw a picture of what happens to rocks that a river carries into the ocean.

What else might happen to rocks when they are swept into the ocean?

Color to reflect on your learning.

Lesson Review

1

- ◯ The stream is carrying small rocks.
- ◯ The stream is carrying soil particles.
- ◯ The stream is moving quickly.

2

- ◯ slow change
- ◯ fast change

3

- ◯ water
- ◯ sunlight
- ◯ wind

DIRECTIONS 1. Which sentence best explains why this stream is brown? Check the box. 2. Which type of change is shown in the photo? Check the box. 3. What might cause the sand to move on this beach? Check two boxes. SC.1.E.6.3

PAGE KEELEY SCIENCE PROBES

Quick Changes to Earth's Surface

Shestin

Look at that landslide! I think landslides and earthquakes make quick changes to Earth's surface.

Karima

I think erosion makes quick changes to Earth's surface.

Rae

I think landslides, earthquakes, floods, and volcanoes make quick changes.

Pierre

I agree with everyone. All of these things cause quick changes.

DIRECTIONS Who do you agree with? Circle their picture or name.
Talk About It Explain your thinking.

Essential Question

How can Earth's surface change quickly?

Watch *When the Ground Moves*

Hands-On Investigation

Model Fast Changes to Earth

SC.1.N.1.1 SC.1.N.1.3

Get your notebook and go explore!

Quick Changes

Earth's surface can change. Sometimes the changes happen **quickly**. An earthquake happens when two parts of Earth move. This makes the ground shake. Earthquakes can break big rocks, or even roads, quickly.

A volcano is an opening in Earth's surface. When a volcano erupts, gases and lava are forced out. What does the lava look like in this photo?

DIRECTIONS Think about the Model Fast Changes to Earth investigation. Now, read to learn more.

Lava is hot when it moves over land. When it cools, it turns into rock. Lava changes Earth's surface quickly.

A landslide happens when soil and rocks fall from higher to lower ground. This could happen down a hill or mountain. Changes from landslides happen very quickly.

Investigation Connection How did a tap affect your model? Did a twist have a different effect?
Talk About It Describe the changes in the photos. Do any of the photos show similar changes? Explain your thinking.

Changes from Water

A flood happens when water flows over land and cannot easily soak into the ground. A flood can happen after it rains. A flood can happen with strong waves.

Rivers can flood. Lakes can flood. Even oceans can flood. A flood can quickly change the surface of Earth. How is the flood in this photo changing the surface?

Why would it be helpful to know about a flooded road?

Fast Changes to Earth's Surface

Photo	Description	Fast Change
		earthquake
	water flows over land	
		landslide
	lava flows over land	

Watch *Quick Change.*

Investigation Connection Review the results of the investigation. Which type of change happened to your model? Was it a slow change or a fast change?

DIRECTIONS **Read the Table** Observe each photo in the table. Complete the table. Write the type of fast change or describe the fast change.

Observe Your World

The village was covered in lava. No one was hurt.

A Volcano Grows

Long ago, a farmer in Mexico saw a hole in his field. Smoke and lava were coming out of it! The lava got hard and turned into rock. It grew into a volcano almost 1,000 feet tall! It took ten years to form the Paricutin Volcano.

Watch *Eruption!*

Write About It! Draw a picture of an erupting volcano. Use words from the Interactive Word Wall to label your picture. ELA.K12.EE.1.1

Am I Ready?

Draw before-and-after pictures of a fast change to Earth's surface.

How did Earth's surface change in the picture you drew?

Color to reflect on your learning.

Lesson Review

1

☐ slow change

☐ fast change

2

☐ Water flows over land and cannot easily soak into the ground.

☐ Melted rock flows over land and changes Earth's surface.

3

☐ earthquake

☐ volcano

☐ flood

DIRECTIONS 1. Observe the photo. Is the landslide a slow change or a fast change? Check the box. 2. Which sentence explains the fast change shown in the photo? Check the box. 3. Which fast change happens when two parts of Earth move? Check the box. SC.1.E.6.3

CHAPTER 4

Living and Nonliving Things Are Connected

Check it out!

Do turtles need plants?

SC.1.L.14.1 Make observations of living things and their environment using the five senses.

SC.1.L.14.2 Identify the major parts of plants, including stem, roots, leaves, and flowers.

SC.1.L.14.3 Differentiate between living and nonliving things.

SC.1.L.17.1 Through observation, recognize that all plants and animals, including humans, need the basic necessities of air, water, food, and space.

Chapter Preview

Take Note!

DIRECTIONS What did you see in the video that interested you? Draw a picture.

PAGE KEELEY SCIENCE PROBES

Living Things

dog

manatee

tree

flowers

fire

river

stick

grass

bike

DIRECTIONS Circle the photos of things that are living.
Talk About It What did you circle? Why? Show a partner.

Essential Question

How do you classify living and nonliving things?

Watch *Puppy Play.*

Hands-On Investigation

Classify Things

SC.1.N.1.2 SC.1.N.1.4

Get your notebook and go explore!

Living and Nonliving

You can classify things as living or nonliving. Living things grow, change, and have needs. A penguin is a living thing.

Living things have **basic needs**. Basic needs help living things grow and stay alive. Food and water are basic needs.

Living things **produce young**. This means they make offspring. Plants produce young called seedlings.

DIRECTIONS Think about the Classify Things investigation. Now, read to learn more.

Nonliving things do not grow, change, or have needs. A cloud is a nonliving thing.

Nonliving things do not have basic needs. A marble is a nonliving thing.

Nonliving things do not produce young. A rock is a nonliving thing.

Watch *Is It Living?*

Quick Lab Get ready to explore. SC.1.N.1.3 SC.1.N.1.4

Investigation Connection Look at your investigation. Did you list some senses more than others?

Use Your Senses to Observe

Animals use their senses to observe the world around them. People do too.
We collect information using different parts of our bodies.

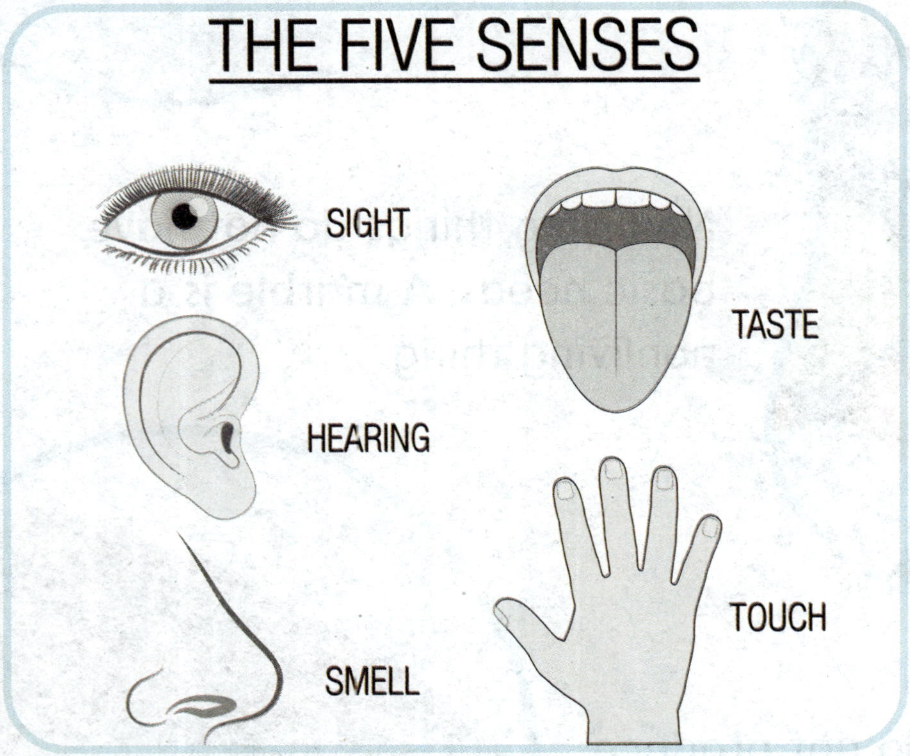

You use your senses of touch, taste, and sight.
You use your senses of smell and hearing, too.

Which senses are being used in this photo?

Is a turtle living or nonliving? How do you know?

Use Your Senses to Identify

Elephants are living things.
They have basic needs.
They eat plants and drink water.
Elephants can produce young called calves.

Water is a nonliving thing.
It does not have basic needs.
Water does not produce young.

DIRECTIONS **Read the Photo** 1. Draw a circle around the living things in the photo. 2. Draw a check mark on the nonliving things in the photo.
Talk About It Think about the five senses. Which senses can you use to identify living things and where they live? Share your answers with a partner.

Build Your Skill

Take a Closer Look

1. Go outside.
2. Listen to your teacher.
3. Look for living things. Look for nonliving things.
4. Use your five senses as you look.

DIRECTIONS Apply It Observe the living and nonliving things you find. SC.1.N.1.3
Write About It! Draw and label your observations.
What did you observe with your five senses?

Use words from the Interactive Word Wall to label your picture. ELA.K12.EE.5.1

Am I Ready?

Draw a living thing.

What makes this a living thing?

Color to reflect on your learning.

Lesson Review

1

2

- [ ] It does not grow.
- [ ] It produces young.
- [ ] It does not have basic needs.

3

- [ ] taste
- [ ] hearing

DIRECTIONS 1. Circle the living things. Draw an X on the nonliving things. 2. What makes something a living thing? Check the box. 3. Which of the senses is the monkey using? Check the box.

SC.1.L.14.1 SC.1.L.14.3

PAGE KEELEY SCIENCE PROBES

What Do They Both Need?

water

food

space

sunlight

soil

air

DIRECTIONS Circle the things all plants and animals need to live.
Talk About It What did you circle? Think carefully about what all plants and animals need, not just some.

Essential Question

What do plants and animals need?

Watch *Lurking Lion.*

Lesson 2

Cape Canaveral, FL

Hands-On Investigation

Research Living Things

SC.1.N.1.1 SC.1.N.1.3

Get your notebook and go explore!

Read Together

Plant and Animal Needs

All living things need water, food, air, and space. These things help plants, animals, and humans live and grow.

People and animals drink water. They also get water when they eat some foods.

Plants get water from the ground. They also get water from rain. People water plants too.

DIRECTIONS Think about the Research Living Things investigation. Now, read to learn more.

People and animals eat food for energy. Energy helps people run, play, live, and grow.

Plants need sunlight, water, and air to make food. Plants grow where they can get what they need to live. What have you noticed about where plants live?

Investigation Connection Think about your research. Have you learned more about how to take care of a plant or an animal?

Space to Live

Plants and animals live in different places. Some live on land. Others live in water. Plants and animals need **space** to live and grow.

Some plants only need a little space. Some plants, like trees, need a lot of space.

People and animals use spaces that are safe and warm. These spaces are **shelters.** Some animals find shelter under rocks, behind plants, or in homes. Can you think of a space that can provide shelter?

What are a turtle's needs?

People and animals need air to breathe and **survive.**

Everglades National Park, FL

Plants need air to make food.

Fish have gills for taking in air under water. Dolphins have blowholes for breathing above water.

DIRECTIONS How can your senses help you observe how animals breathe?
Talk About It What senses help you observe where animals live?

STEM Connection IF/THEN

This Is What A Scientist Looks Like®

Meet a Photographer

Jenny Adler is a scientist.
She studies where animals live.
She takes photos under the water.
The photos show where animals live.
Which of her five senses could Jenny use under the water?

The animals need clean water.
The animals need food.
The photos show how animals live.
The photos teach us about animals.

Look at the crayfish!
It lives in the water.

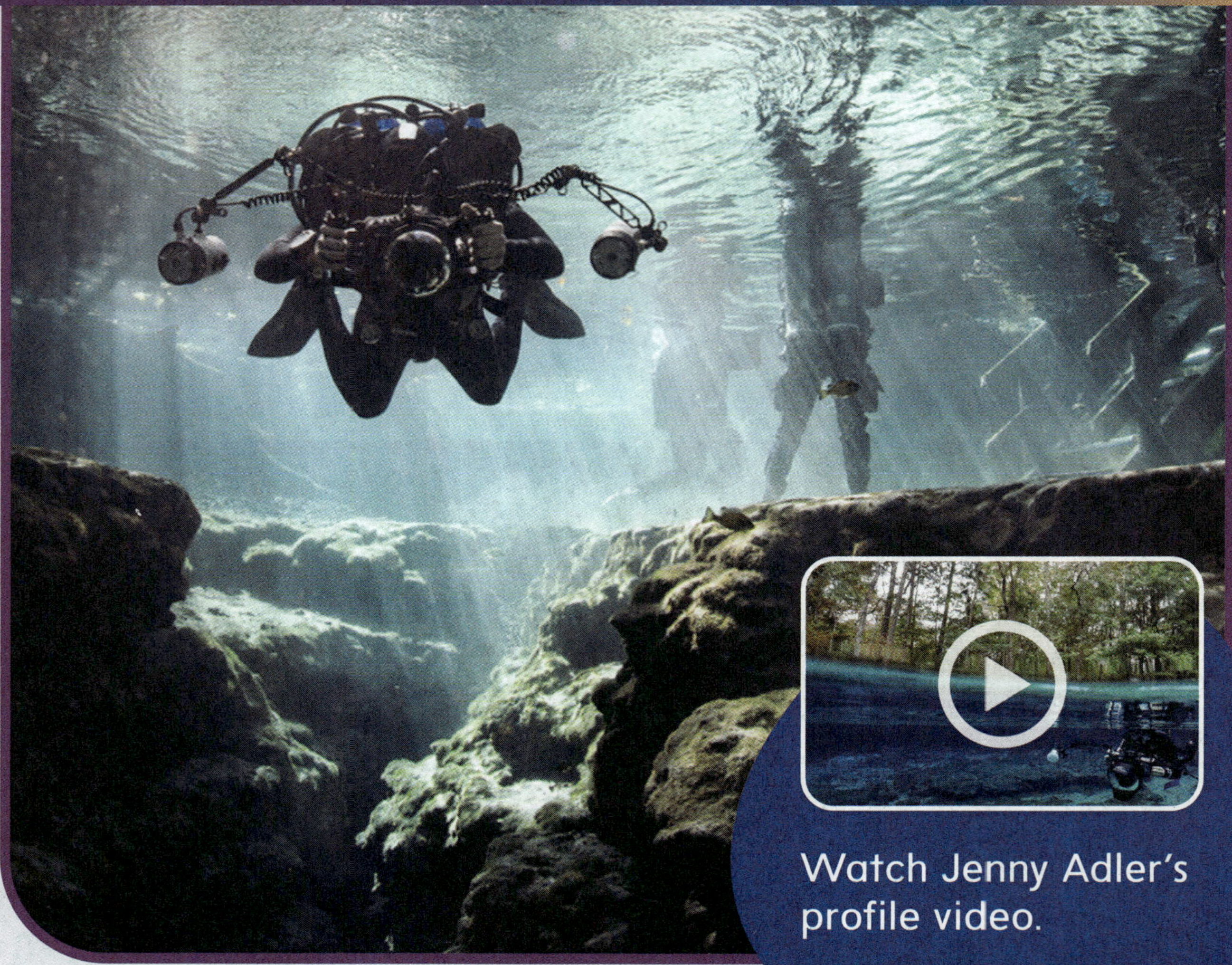

Watch Jenny Adler's profile video.

Write About It!

What does your favorite animal need? Organize your information.

Topic and Details

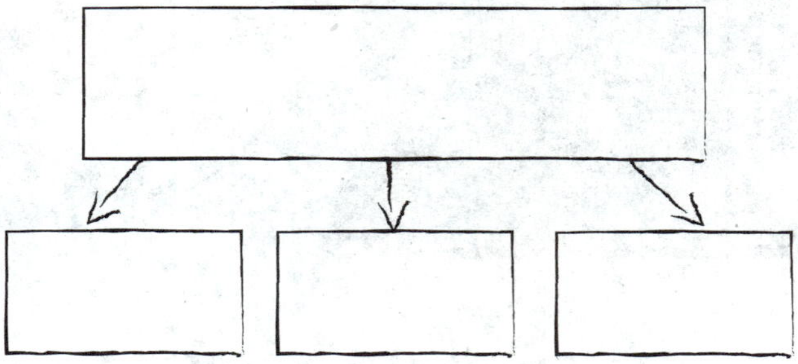

Write About It! What are the needs of your favorite animal? Draw a picture.

Use words from the Interactive Word Wall to label the needs of your favorite animal. ELA.K12.EE.5.1

Am I Ready?

Draw a plant or an animal with something it needs to live and grow.

What other basic needs could you have drawn?

Color to reflect on your learning.

Lesson Review

1

2

- [ ] water
- [ ] space
- [ ] food

3

- [ ] sunlight
- [ ] air
- [ ] water

DIRECTIONS 1. Which two photos show the same basic need? Circle the photos. 2. The tree is in an open field. What need does that meet? Check the box. 3. What basic need are the children giving the plants? Check the box. SC.1.L.14.1 SC.1.L.17.1

PAGE KEELEY SCIENCE PROBES

Plant Parts

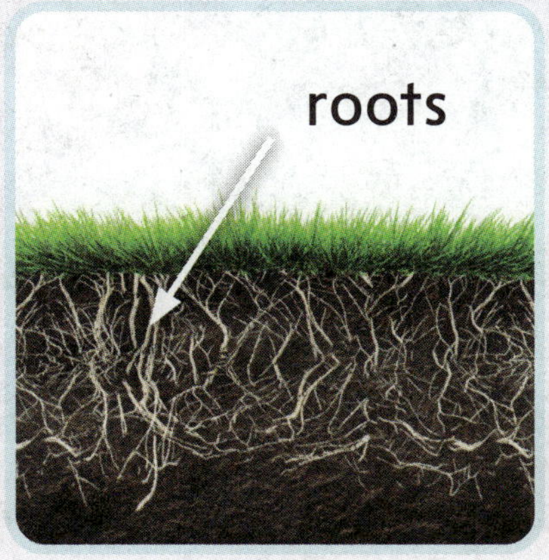

DIRECTIONS Circle the pictures that show major parts of plants.
Talk About It What did you circle? Why? Show a partner.

Essential Question

What are some plant structures?

▶ Watch *Terrific Tomatoes.*

Hands-On Investigation

Plenty of Plant Parts

SC.1.N.1.3

Get your notebook and go explore!

Plants Have Parts

Plants have **structures.**
A structure is a part of something.

A **leaf** is a plant structure.

A **stem** is a plant structure.

Roots are plant structures.
Roots grow under the ground.

DIRECTIONS Think about the Plenty of Plant Parts investigation. Now, read to learn more.

A **flower** is another plant structure.
Flowers have many colors, shapes, and sizes.

A **fruit** holds the plant's seeds.
Some fruits are good to eat!

DIRECTIONS **Read the Diagram** 1. Use a red crayon to circle the roots.
2. Use a blue crayon to circle the seeds.
Talk About It What else can you learn about plant structures by looking at the diagram?
Which of your five senses do you use when you eat?

Different Plants

A tree trunk is a stem.
We get wood from tree trunks.

A cactus has a thick, green stem. It does not have green leaves.

Some stems can climb fences. Ivy can climb walls!

Which parts of a plant might a turtle need?

A water lily has wide, flat leaves. Water lily leaves float!

The leaves on pine trees are long and thin. They are called needles.

Carrots are roots we eat. Potatoes are roots too.

Watch *Parts of a Plant.*

Investigation Connection Compare the plant structures you observed in the investigation to the plant structures shown in this lesson.

Talk About It Which of your five senses could help you learn about stems?

Build Your Skill

Plant Problem

Think about what you know about the needs of living things.

1 Observe the photo of the sunflower.

2 Define a problem that you see.

3 Propose a solution to solve the problem.

DIRECTIONS Apply It 1. What problem does the plant have? 2. How could you solve the problem? SC.1.N.1.2

Write About It! Draw and label your solution.

Use words from the Interactive Word Wall to label the parts of the plant. ELA.K12.EE.1.1

Am I Ready?

Draw and label three plant structures.

Describe one of the plant structures you drew.

Color to reflect on your learning.

Lesson Review

1

2

☐ stem

☐ flower

3

DIRECTIONS 1. Circle the plant structure that grows under the ground. 2. Which plant structure is circled? Check the box. 3. Circle the structure that holds the plant's seeds. SC.1.L.14.1 SC.1.L.14.2

CHAPTER 5

Plant and Animal Observations

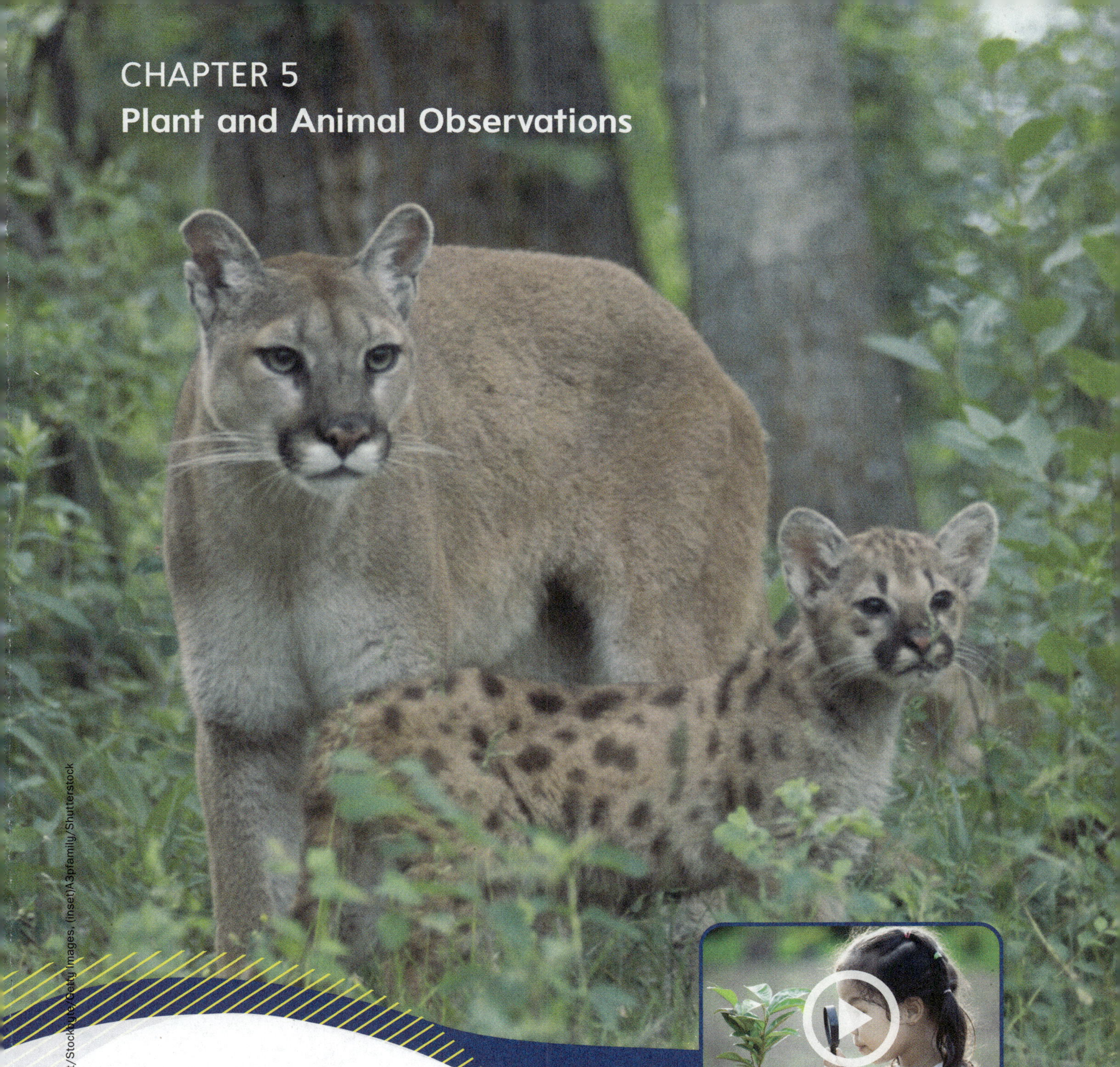

Check it out!

How are these living things alike?

SC.1.L.14.1 Make observations of living things and their environment using the five senses.

SC.1.L.16.1 Make observations that plants and animals closely resemble their parents, but variations exist among individuals within a population.

Chapter Preview

Take Note!

DIRECTIONS What did you see in the video that interested you? Draw a picture.

PAGE KEELEY SCIENCE PROBES

Young Plants

Joyce

It was great visiting the garden today. There were a lot of young plants. I think young plants look exactly like their parents.

Melinda

I think young plants look like their parents but can have some differences.

I think young plants look very different from their parents.

Kai

DIRECTIONS Circle who you agree with.
Talk About It Who did you circle? Why? Show a partner.

Essential Question

Do all young plants look like their parents?

Watch *Cactus Family.*

Hands-On Investigation

Plant Walk

SC.1.N.1.1 SC.1.N.1.2 SC.1.N.1.3

Get your notebook and go explore!

Young Plants and Parents

Many living things look like their **parents**. Some young plants look and grow like their parents.

Not all plants look just like their parents. They can even look different from each other.

Young plants change as they grow. What changes do you notice?

DIRECTIONS Think about the Plant Walk investigation. Now, read to learn more.

The way plants look and grow are called **traits.** Young plants inherit traits. To inherit means to get a trait from a parent.

Their flowers may have the same shape or color. This means they have similar traits.

The shape of a leaf is a good example. It is an inherited trait.

Investigation Connection Review the results from the investigation. What traits did each plant have?

Talk About It Do you think the plants you observed in the investigation are a young plant and its parent? Share your thoughts with a partner.

Compare Plants

Some young plants look different from their parent plants. They can even look different from other plants with the same name.

young ferns

fern parents

The fern parent plants might not look exactly like each other. Do they look like the young ferns?

How are the plants alike? What senses can you use to observe them?

Look at the corn plants and tomato plants. Observe the young plant. Observe the parent.

corn plants

tomato plants

Compare the young plant to its parent plant. Which traits are similar and different?

Talk About It Look at the size, shape, color, and plant structures of the young plants in the top row. Compare the young plants to their parent plants in the bottom row. Talk to a partner about the differences you observe.

STEM Connection

GrowNYC

Volunteers plant gardens.
First, they prepare the soil.
Next, they plant fruits and vegetables.
Then, they sell the fruits and vegetables.

GrowNYC fixes empty spaces in the city.
Volunteers clean up the spaces.
Volunteers help people too!

Watch *GrowNYC.*

GrowNYC plants school gardens.
Students learn how to plant gardens.
They grow fruits and vegetables in soil.

Write About It!

What would you grow in your garden? Use the Word Web to organize your information.

Write About It! What type of plants would you grow in a garden? Would you grow flowers, fruit, or vegetables? Discuss with a partner. Share your plans and listen to your partner's ideas. Then, draw and label a picture of your garden.

Use words from the Interactive Word Wall to label your garden. ELA.K12.EE.4.1

Am I Ready?

Draw a young plant and its parent plant. Label something that is the same and something that is different.

What is the same and what is different about the two plants you drew?

Color to reflect on your learning.

Lesson Review

1

- [ ] yes
- [ ] no

2

- [ ] parents
- [ ] sunlight
- [ ] soil

3

- [ ] soil
- [ ] leaf shape
- [ ] sunlight

DIRECTIONS 1. Do young plants always look exactly like their parents? Check the box. 2. Where do plants inherit their traits from? 3. Which is a plant trait? Check the box. SC.1.L.16.1

PAGE KEELEY SCIENCE PROBES

Puppies

Shestin

Big news! My dog Maggie is going to have puppies soon!

Karima

I think Maggie's puppies will look exactly like her.

Rae

I think the puppies will look similar to Maggie, but not the same.

Pierre

I don't think Maggie's puppies will look like her.

DIRECTIONS Circle who you agree with.
Talk About It Who did you circle? Why? Show a partner.

Essential Question

How are young animals similar to their parents?

Watch *Part of the Pack.*

Hands-On Investigation

Match Parent and Young

SC.1.N.1.2 SC.1.N.1.3

Get your notebook and go explore!

Parents and Their Young

Many young animals resemble their parents. To **resemble** means to look like something.

A baby giraffe resembles its parent. Both have long necks. A young zebra has black and white stripes. Its parent has stripes too.

DIRECTIONS Think about the Match Parent and Young investigation. Now, read to learn more.
Talk About It How can your senses help you observe young animals and their parents?

How do these kittens resemble the parent cat? Each kitten has two eyes, four legs, and a tail. They all have soft fur that covers their bodies.

Penguin chicks resemble their parents too. The chicks have short wings and walk on two legs. They have black and white coloring on their bodies, just like their parents.

These young resemble their parents. Can you guess what animal they are?

Investigation Connection In the investigation, how did the young animals look similar to and different from their parents?

Compare Animals

Young animals can look different from their siblings and parents. Young animals begin their lives smaller than their parents. They may have other differences too. Compare the vulture chick to its parent.

Puppies resemble their parents. Do all puppies look alike? What differences do you notice?

Watch *Animal Families.*

How are the panthers alike? What senses help you make observations?

Quick Lab Get ready to explore. SC.1.N.1.3

How Do They Compare?

DIRECTIONS Read the Photo 1. Match each animal parent with its young by drawing a line to connect them. 2. Tell a partner how the young animal resembles its parent.

Talk About It Can you think of another young animal that resembles its parents?

Observe Your World

Different for a Good Reason

Young animals resemble their parents. But they are not exactly alike. Lion cubs have spots. This is for a good reason. When adult lions go hunting, they leave their cubs behind. The cubs' spots help them stay hidden and safe while they are alone.

The lion and her cubs are similar, but different.

Watch
Spot the Cub.

Write About It! Draw and label a picture of a young animal that resembles its parent.

Use words from the Interactive Word Wall to label your picture. ELA.K12.EE.2.1

Am I Ready?

Draw and label a picture of an animal parent and its young.

What animal and its young did you draw? How are they alike?

Color to reflect on your learning.

Lesson Review

1

2

- [ ] They are the same size.
- [ ] They have beaks.
- [ ] They are the same color.

3

DIRECTIONS 1. Which animal resembles the calf? Circle it. 2. How are the baby swans like the mother swan? Check the correct answer. 3. Which animal could be the young of the adult tiger? Circle it. SC.1.L.16.1

Check it out!

How are toys unique?

SC.1.P.8.1 Sort objects by observable properties, such as size, shape, color, temperature (hot or cold), weight (heavy or light), texture, and whether objects sink or float.

Chapter Preview

Let's learn!

Take Note!

DIRECTIONS What did you see in the video that interested you? Draw a picture.

PAGE KEELEY SCIENCE PROBES

Properties of Objects

How big is it?	What shape is it?
What does it feel like?	How pretty is it?
How heavy is it?	What color is it?
How much does it cost?	Who uses it?

DIRECTIONS Circle the questions you can use to describe the physical properties of an object.
Talk About It What did you circle? Why? Show a partner.

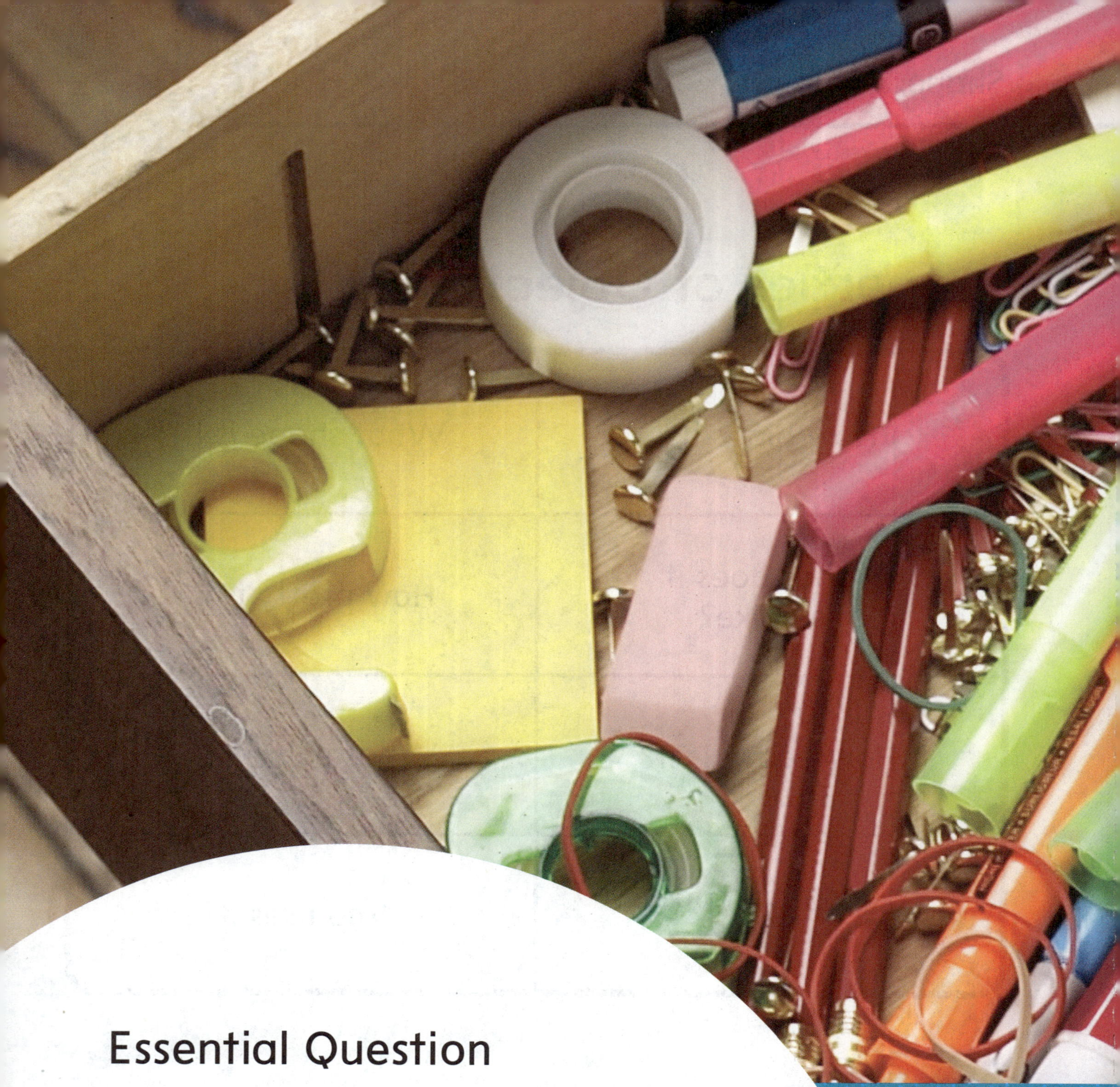

Essential Question

How can objects be classified by property?

Watch *Snazzy Supplies.*

Hands-On Investigation

Super Sorters

SC.1.N.1.2 SC.1.N.1.3

Get your notebook and go explore!

Let's Classify

An **object** is anything that can be seen and touched. Every object has properties.

Physical properties are ways to describe objects and tell them apart. Two properties are **color** and **shape**.

You can see color and shape.
Which foods are yellow?
Which foods have a tube shape?
Classify them!

DIRECTIONS Think about the Super Sorters investigation. Now, read to learn more.

Texture is how something feels. You can use touch to tell shape and texture. The texture of an object can be soft or hard. It also can be smooth, bumpy, or sharp.

Texture can be useful for classifying animals. How are these animals alike and different?

What examples of colors, shapes, and textures do you see in this photo?

Investigation Connection What senses did you use to classify objects during the investigation? Which sense was the most useful for you? Why?

More Properties

Temperature is how hot or cold something is. You can sort objects by temperature.

You can use your sense of touch to observe temperature. What other senses can you use?

Food can be hot or cold. Weather can be hot or cold too. What examples of temperature do you see in these photos?

Talk About It Discuss the photos with a partner. What properties do you observe in each photo?

Can some toys be hot or cold?

Objects that **float** stay near the surface of water. Have you ever seen an object float?

Objects that **sink** go down below the surface of water. What senses can you use to tell if something is floating or sinking?

DIRECTIONS Read the Photo 1. Draw a circle around the objects that float in water.
2. Draw a check mark on the objects that sink in water.

Quick Lab Get ready to explore. SC.1.N.1.2 SC.1.N.1.3

STEM Connection IF/THEN

This Is What A Scientist Looks Like®

Meet a Maker and 3D Printer

When Karina Popovich was little, she liked to play with tools. She liked to build things. She spent a lot of time building and making things.

She is studying to be an engineer. Engineers use models. She makes models with a 3D printer.

You can use a 3D printer to print all kinds of things. You can print with different colors. You can make many shapes and textures!

First, you use a computer. You make a design. Next, you use a 3D printer. It makes thin layers from plastic. Then, it combines the layers.

Watch *Camp GoldieBlox: Karina Popovich.*

Doctors and nurses needed face shields. Karina Popovich printed face shields with pink and blue ear savers to prevent irritation.

Write About It!

What problem did Karina Popovich help solve with her 3D printer? Organize your information.

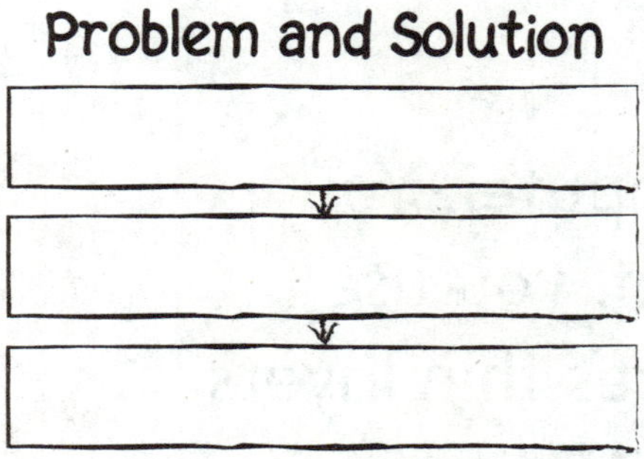

Write About It! Draw and label a picture of Karina Popovich's solutions. Organize your information using the problem and solution graphic organizer. Write a short response about her solution.

Use words from the Interactive Word Wall to label your drawings and write your sentence. ELA.K12.EE.2.1

Am I Ready?

Draw two toys with different properties.

Tell about the properties of the toys.

Color to reflect on your learning.

Lesson Review

1

☐  ☐ 

☐  ☐ 

2

☐ color

☐ float or sink

☐ hot or cold

3

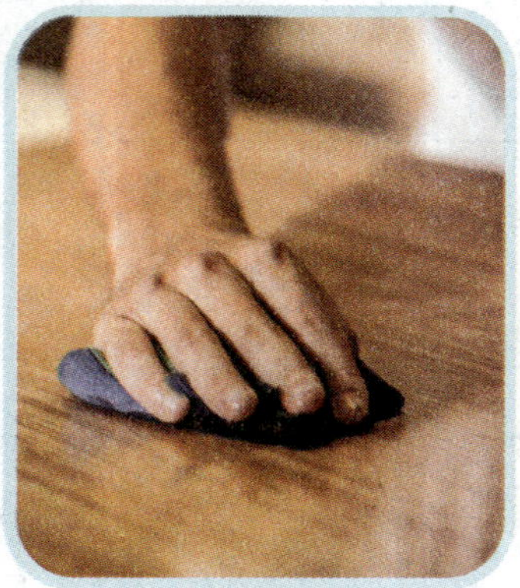

☐ The table is smooth and hard.

☐ The table is soft and bumpy.

☐ The table is rough and hard.

☐ The table is smooth and soft.

DIRECTIONS 1. Classify the shapes. Which shape belongs in this group? Check the box.
2. Which property was used to sort the objects? Check the box.
3. What is the texture of the table in the photo? Check the box. SC.1.P.8.1

PAGE KEELEY SCIENCE PROBES

Are Big Things Heavier than Small Things?

Lily

Mr. Lei said he needs help carrying boxes. Do you think they will be too big to carry? ☆

Pia

I think size doesn't matter in how heavy things are.

I think big things are heavier than small things. ☆

Lily

DIRECTIONS Circle the photo of the student you agree with.
Talk About It Who did you circle? Why? Show a partner.

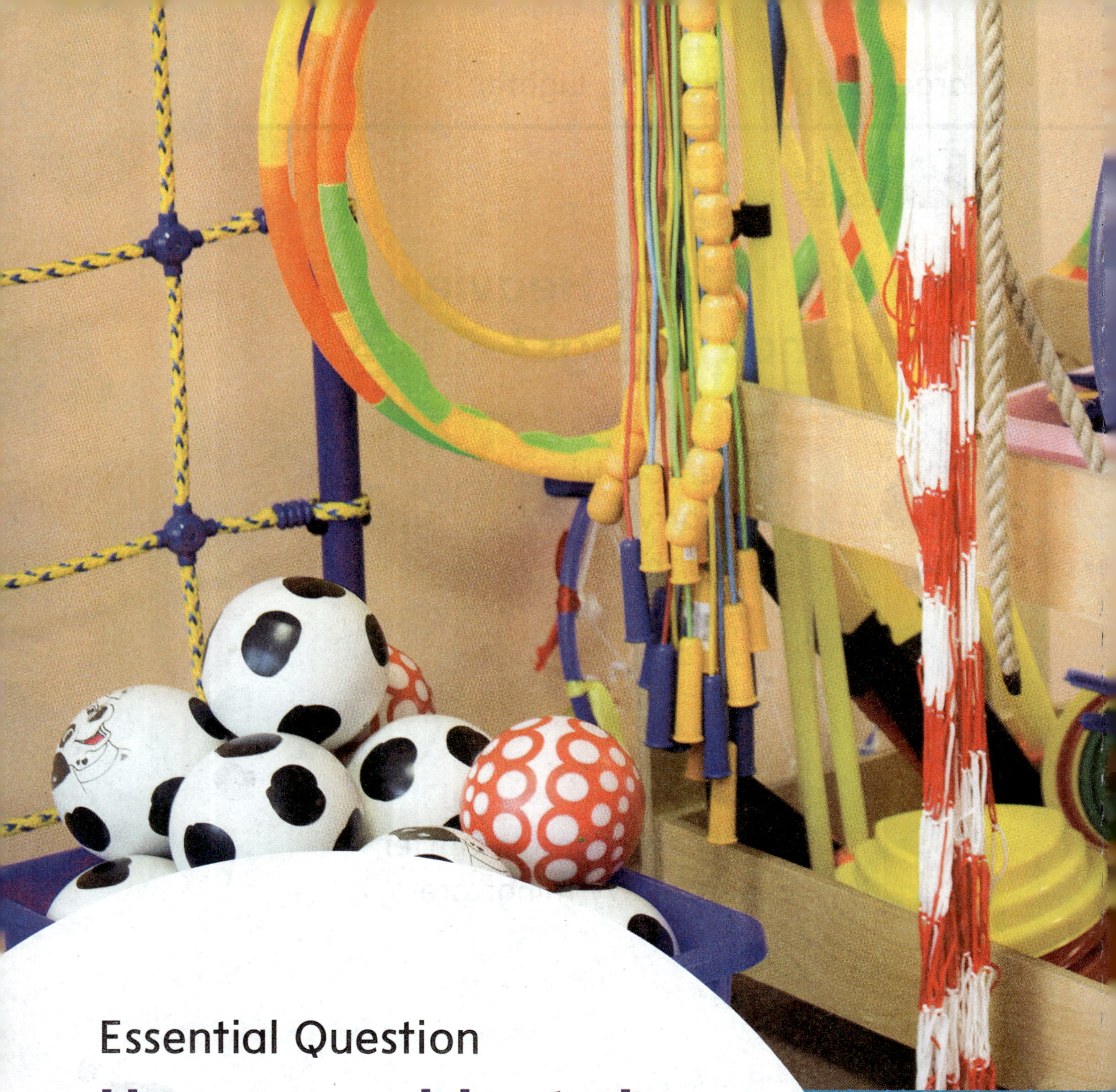

Essential Question

How can objects be classified by size?

Watch *Spot the Difference.*

Hands-On Investigation

Size Surprise

SC.1.N.1.2 SC.1.N.1.3

Get your notebook and go explore!

Classify More

Size is how large or small something is. It is a physical property. We use describing words to tell how large or small. These are **attributes**. Attributes help describe the properties of objects.

What do you observe about the dog and cat? What attributes would you use to describe them?

DIRECTIONS Think about the Size Surprise investigation. Now, read to learn more.

Quick Lab Get ready to explore. SC.1.N.1.2 SC.1.N.1.3

Sometimes, smaller objects are heavier than larger objects. The stack of books is small and heavy. The box is large and light.

The horse is big, brown, and heavy. The apple is small, yellow, and light.

Watch *Classify Objects.*

Investigation Connection Look at the data table from the investigation. What did you notice about the size and weight of the objects?

Compare Attributes

You can compare the sizes of objects with your senses. Compare the bear and the clock. Which object is smaller?

You can compare how heavy objects are by using a balance. The lower side has the heavier object. The higher side has the lighter object.

How can comparing attributes help you classify objects?

Talk About It Which is heavier, the popcorn or the marbles? Share your thinking with a partner.

How can toys be classified according to size and heaviness?

DIRECTIONS Read the Photo 1. Think about the attributes of the objects in the photos. 2. Work with a partner. Choose one photo. What are two ways you can sort the objects in the photo?

Build Your Skill

Use a Balance

1

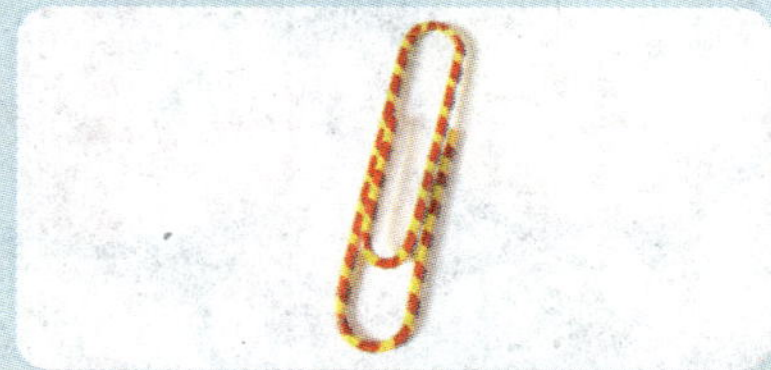

2

3

DIRECTIONS Apply It 1. Circle the heavier object. 2. Circle the heavier object. 3. Circle the lighter object. Compare your observations with a partner. SC.1.N.1.2

Write About It! Draw and label a picture of a balance with a heavy object and a lighter object. Use words from the Interactive Word Wall to label your picture. ELA.K12.EE.5.1

Am I Ready?

Draw two objects that have different attributes. Classify and label them.

How are the objects different?

Color to reflect on your learning.

Lesson Review

1

- [ ] crayon
- [ ] toy car

2

3

cup egg bowl book

DIRECTIONS 1. Which object is heavier? Check the box. 2. Draw an object that is smaller than the ladybug. 3. Classify the objects. Circle the two smallest objects. SC.1.P.8.1

CHAPTER 7

Forces and Motion

Check it out!

What's happening at the water park?

SC.1.P.12.1 Demonstrate and describe the various ways that objects can move, such as in a straight line, zigzag, back-and-forth, round-and-round, fast, and slow.

SC.1.P.13.1 Demonstrate that the way to change the motion of an object is by applying a push or a pull.

Chapter Preview

Let's learn!

Take Note!

DIRECTIONS What did you see in the video that interested you? Draw a picture.

PAGE KEELEY SCIENCE PROBES

Changes to Motion

going faster	slowing down
turning around	stopping
going backward	starting up
going sideways	zig zagging

DIRECTIONS Circle examples of ways that objects can move.
Talk About It What did you circle? Why? Show a partner.

Essential Question

How do pushes and pulls change the motion of an object?

Watch *Move and Groove.*

Lesson I

Hands-On Investigation

Marble Motion

SC.1.N.1.1 SC.1.N.1.3

Get your notebook and go explore!

Pushes and Pulls

Do you like playing with toys that move? You use **pushes** and **pulls** to move toys and other things.

push

pull

A push moves something away from you. A pull moves something toward you. Pushes and pulls can change how things move.

Pushes and pulls make things move. When an object moves, its position changes. It is put into **motion**.

motion

What kinds of pushes and pulls do you see at a water park?

A push or pull can stop an object's motion.

The child kicks the ball. Another child gives it a push, or kick. The ball stops rolling.

Everything moves with **speed** and **direction.** Speed measures how fast or slow an object is moving. Direction is the path on which something moves.

DIRECTIONS Think about the Marble Motion investigation. Now, read to learn more.

Let's Play

Do you like being pushed on a swing? Each push makes your speed faster. Your direction changes between forward and backward, and up and down.

Check out
Different Forces.

DIRECTIONS Read the Photo In each photo, circle an object that is moving. Draw an arrow to show how the moving object is pushing another object.

Pushes and pulls are part of every sport. They can put a ball into motion. They also change the position of the ball. You can push a sports ball in many ways. In soccer, a net catches the ball.

A kick is a push from your foot. You catch a ball with a push from your hands.

You can even push a ball with your head!

Investigation Connection Did the marbles change speed or direction? Did they change both speed and direction?
Talk About It Share your thinking with a partner.

STEM Connection

Meet an Engineer

Katherine Johnson was a mathematician. She was also a scientist. She knew all about pushes and pulls. When a spaceship blasts off, it pushes off the ground.

Katherine used this information when she worked. She planned NASA's first trip to the Moon! She also planned a spaceship's journey around Earth.

Meet an Astronaut

Years later, Sally Ride got a job at NASA. She was a scientist. She was also an astronaut. Sally was the first American woman in space! The spaceship she was on used pushes and pulls to change direction and stay in motion.

Watch *Meet an Engineer and an Astronaut.*

Write About It!

How does someone at NASA use pushes and pulls? Organize your information.

T-Chart

Write About It! Write about the different ways pushes and pulls are used. Draw a picture. ELA.K12.EE.1.1

Use words from the Interactive Word Wall to label your picture and write your sentence.

Am I Ready?

Draw yourself playing a game where you have to push or pull a ball.

Describe what you drew.

Color to reflect on your learning.

Lesson Review

1

2

- [ ] Iris will go faster.
- [ ] Iris will go slower.

3

- [ ] a push
- [ ] a pull

DIRECTIONS 1. Which drawings show a push? Circle each push. Which drawings show a pull? Draw an X over each pull. 2. Iris is getting pushed on her scooter. How will the push change her speed? Check the box. 3. What does the photo show? Check the box. SC.1.P.12.1 SC.1.P.13.1

PAGE KEELEY SCIENCE PROBES

Skateboarding

DIRECTIONS Circle who you agree with.
Talk About It Who did you circle? Why? Show a partner.

Essential Question

How do you plan and conduct an investigation?

Watch *Let's Investigate.*

Hands-On Investigation

Move the Car

SC.1.N.1.1

Get your notebook and go explore!

Can a Push Change Motion?

Follow along as the students plan and conduct an investigation.

How can pushing a ball change the speed of its motion? We predict that a big push will make the ball move faster than a small push.

1. Ask

2. Plan

We think of ways to test our question. We plan the steps.

DIRECTIONS **Read the Infographic** Learn how to conduct an investigation. Record your observations by drawing a picture that explains what you see.

3. Conduct

We **apply** a push to the ball to see what happens!

4. Observe

We observe the speed of the ball. We test three different pushes.

5. Record

We record what we observe each time.

6. Communicate

We share what we learned. A bigger push can make a ball move faster.

DIRECTIONS Think about the Move the Car investigation. Now, read to learn more.

How can you investigate the pushes and pulls at a water park?

Let's Investigate!

How can applying a push change the motion of a toy car? Jayla rolls the car across the floor. Erin pushes the car while it is moving. Erin's push stops the motion of the car.

Investigation Connection Think about the investigation. Do you see pushes and pulls on this page?

Jayla and Erin test what will happen if a moving ball pushes a stopped toy car.

They observe that when the moving ball pushes the toy car, the car is put into motion!

DIRECTIONS Read the Photo Add arrows to the photo to show the motion and direction of the ball and the toy car.

Talk About It You learned two ways a push can change the motion of a toy car. Talk with a partner about another way a push might change the motion of a car.

Build Your Skill

Pushing and Pulling in Everyday Activities

Daisy uses push and pull forces every day.

1. Daisy closes dresser drawers.
2. Daisy plays tug-of-war at recess.
3. Daisy turns light switches off and on.
4. Daisy passes the ball at soccer practice.

DIRECTIONS Apply It 1. Predict whether Daisy uses a push or pull force for each activity. 2. Act out each activity.
Talk About It Talk with a partner about whether you used a push or pull force. SC.1.N.1.1
Write About It! Draw a line down the middle of your paper. On one side of the line, write *push*. On the other side of the line, write *pull*. Draw a picture under the correct side of the paper for each activity you acted out. ELA.K12.EE.5.1
Use words from the Interactive Word Wall to label your picture.

Am I Ready?

Draw a picture of a push changing the motion of an object.

Describe your drawing.

____

____

Color to reflect on your learning.

Lesson Review

1

2

- yes
- no

3

- The bat pulls the ball, putting it into motion.
- The bat pushes the ball, putting it into motion.

DIRECTIONS 1. Which player will kick the ball in the direction that the arrow shows? Circle the player. 2. A ball is rolling across the grass. Can a push or a pull stop the ball? 3. How does the bat change the motion of the ball? SC.1.P.12.1 SC.1.P.13.1

PAGE KEELEY SCIENCE PROBES

Motion and Direction

Pablo

I think objects move in a straight line.

Sofia

I think objects move back-and-forth or round-and-round.

I think objects move in a straight line, back-and-forth, and round-and-round.

Ruthy

DIRECTIONS Circle the person you agree with.
Talk About It Who did you circle? Why? Show a partner.

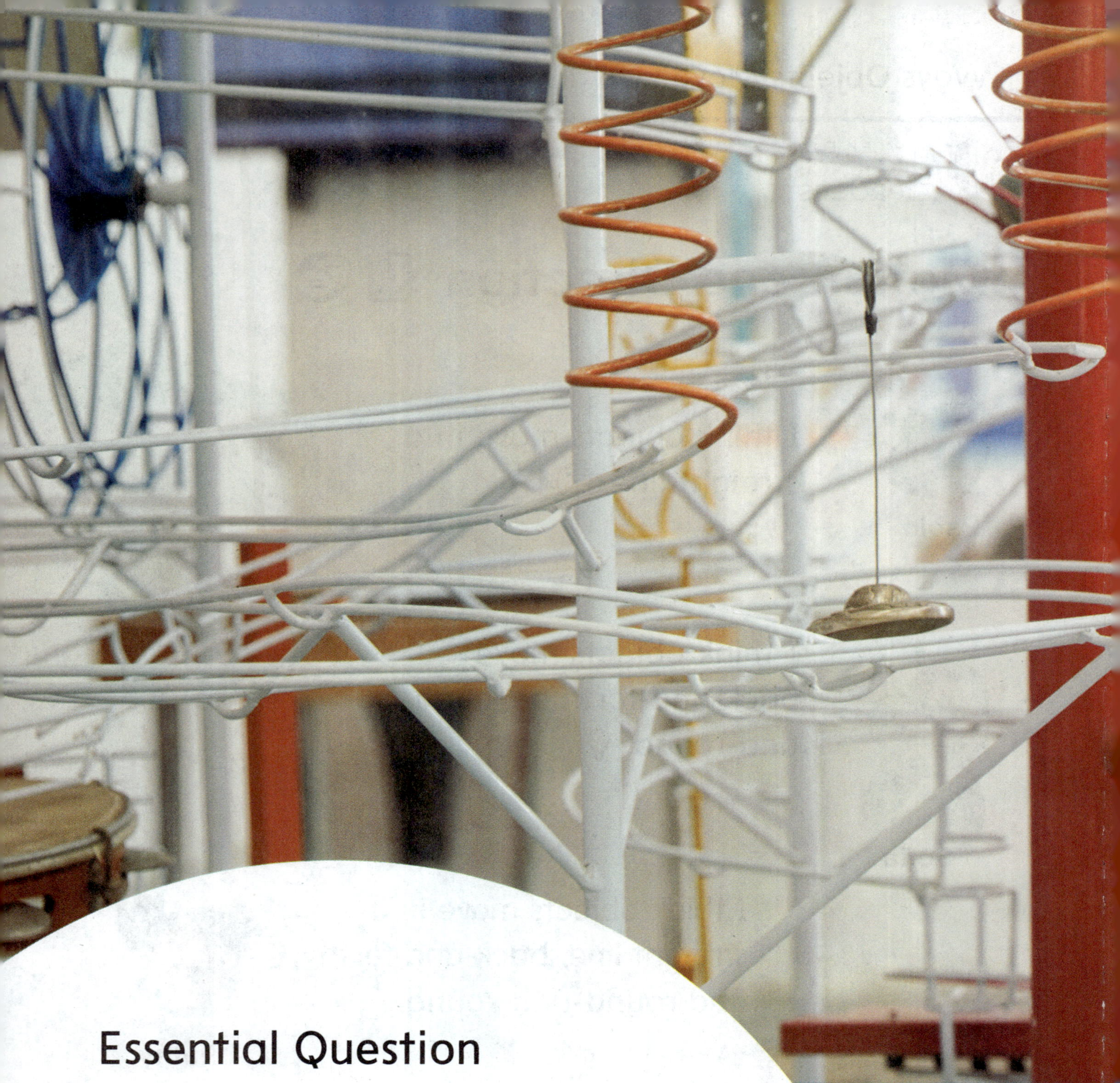

Essential Question

What are the different ways an object can move?

Watch *Super Spinner.*

Hands-On Investigation

Objects in Motion

SC.1.N.1.3

Get your notebook and go explore!

Read Together

Ways Objects Move

What happens when you spin on the playground? You move. When something moves, it changes position.

slow

Things that move are in motion. Motion can be slow or fast. Snails can change position slowly.

fast

Planes are fast. They can change position quickly. What else can change position quickly?

DIRECTIONS Think about the Objects in Motion investigation. Now, read to learn more.

You can describe the motion of an object. You can tell how it changes position. The bowling ball rolls. It moves in a straight line.

straight line

zigzag

A **zigzag** motion moves from side to side. When you walk in zigzags, you make short, sharp turns.

Objects can go back-and-forth. You go back-and-forth when you are on a swing.

back-and-forth

Investigation Connection Think about the investigation. Could some of the objects move in more than one way?
Talk About It What are the advantages of moving in different ways?

How Things Move

Objects can go round-and-round. You can make a toy hoop change speed and direction with your body. Some objects can go up and down. A seesaw goes up and down when you push with your feet.

round-and-round

up and down

Look at the movements of the objects and people in the photos. How do their positions change?

Which of these movements could you see at a water park?

When objects move, they go, go, go.
Some move fast. Some move slow.

FL Tampa, Florida

Look at the photos on the page. Observe how the objects move. Are they fast or slow? In which directions are they moving?

QUICK LAB Get ready to explore. SC.1.N.1.1

Observe Your World

Let's Move!

How are bikes, rides, and a marble run alike?
They all have moving parts.

People look for fun ways to move! They create games and rides that move in many directions. How many ways can these objects move?

In what directions can the ball move?

Write About It! Draw and label a picture of a way you can move your body while dancing. Would you move fast or slow?

Use words from the Interactive Word Wall to label your picture.

ELA.K12.EE.5.1

Am I Ready?

Choose one object that can move in a straight line, zigzag, back-and-forth, or round-and-round motion. Draw a picture.

Describe the movement of the object you drew.

Color to reflect on your learning.

Lesson Review

1

2

- [ ] in a straight line
- [ ] zigzag

3

DIRECTIONS 1. Circle the photo that shows something moving round-and-round. 2. In which direction is the train moving? Check the box. 3. Circle the photo that shows a back-and-forth motion. SC.1.P.12.1

Multilingual Glossary

Looking for multilingual glossaries? Go online to find the glossary in the following languages:

Arabic	French	Portuguese	Urdu
Bengali	Haitian Creole	Russian	Vietnamese
Burmese	Hmong	Swahili	
Chinese	Korean	Tagalog	

A

Español

apply to use — **aplicar** usar

attribute a way to describe a physical property — **atributo** manera de describir una propiedad física

B

basic need what a living thing needs to grow and stay alive — **necesidad básica** lo que un ser vivo necesita para crecer y permanecer con vida

beneficial helpful — **beneficioso** útil

C

change a way of becoming different — **cambiar** manera de volverse diferente

		Español
	**color** one way to describe an object; red and blue are colors	**color** una manera de describir un objeto; el rojo y el azul son colores

D

	**descriptive investigation** steps a scientist takes to answer a question and make a claim	**investigación descriptiva** pasos que sigue un científico para responder una pregunta y hacer una afirmación
	**direction** the path on which something moves	**dirección** curso o trayecto en el que se mueven las cosas

E

	**engineer** a person who identifies problems and designs solutions	**ingeniero** persona que identifica problemas y diseña soluciones

F

	**float** to stay on or near the surface of water or another liquid	**flotar** mantenerse sobre o cerca de la superficie del agua o de otro líquido
	**flower** the plant part that makes seeds	**flor** parte de la planta que produce semillas

Español

fresh water water that has little or no salt in it

agua dulce agua que no tiene sal o tiene poca

fruit plant part that holds the seeds

fruta parte de la planta que contiene las semillas

G

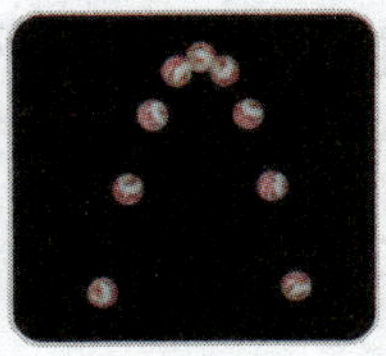

gravity a noncontact force that pulls objects toward the center of Earth

gravedad fuerza de no contacto que atrae los objetos hacia el centro de la Tierra

H

harmful dangerous

dañino peligroso

L

leaf a part of a plant that is often green and flat

hoja parte de la planta que suele ser verde y plana

M

magnify to cause to appear larger

ampliar hacer que un objeto parezca más grande

		Español
	**measure** to find the size or amount of something	**medir** hallar el tamaño o la cantidad de algo
	**motion** a change in an object's position	**movimiento** cambio en la posición de un objeto

N

	**nonliving thing** a thing that does not grow, change, or have needs	**ser inanimado** algo que no crece, no cambia ni tiene necesidades

O

	**object** a thing	**objeto** una cosa
	**organism** a living thing	**organismo** ser vivo que crece, cambia y tiene necesidades

P

	**parent** a living thing that makes young	**progenitor** un ser vivo que produce cría

		Español
	**physical property** anything that can be observed about an object	**propiedad física** todo lo que se puede observar acerca de un objeto
	**problem** a question to be thought about and answered	**problema** cuestión para considerar y responder
	**produce young** to make offspring	**producir retoños** tener hijos
	**prototype** the first model used to solve a problem	**prototipo** el primer modelo usado para resolver un problema
	**pull** to move something closer	**jalar** acercar un objeto
	**push** to move something away	**empujar** alejar algo

Q

	**quickly** in a short time	**rápidamente** en poco tiempo

Glossary · Glosario

R

		Español
	**resemble** to look like	**parecerse** asemejarse
	**rock** a hard, nonliving part of Earth	**roca** parte dura e inanimada de la Tierra
	**root** a part of a plant that grows in the ground	**raíz** parte de la planta que crece debajo del suelo

S

	**salt water** water with salt in it	**agua salada** agua que tiene sal
	**science** using evidence to explain things that happen	**ciencia** usar evidencia para explicar fenómenos que suceden
	**scientist** a person who uses evidence to explain	**científico** persona que explica los fenómenos a partir de evidencia
	**shape** form of an object	**figura** forma de un objeto

		Español
	**shelter** a place for animals to stay safe	**refugio** lugar para que los animales se mantengan seguros
	**sink** to go down below the surface of a liquid	**hundir** sumergir debajo de la superficie de un líquido
	**size** how large or small something is	**tamaño** medida de lo grande o pequeño que es algo
	**slowly** in a long time	**lentamente** en mucho tiempo
	**soil** the top part of the ground where plants grow	**suelo** parte superior de la corteza terrestre en donde crecen las plantas
	**solution** an answer to a problem	**solución** la respuesta a un problema
	**space** an empty area or place	**espacio** área o lugar vacío

		Español
	**speed** how fast or slow an object moves	**velocidad** lo rápido o lento que se mueve un objeto
	**star** an object in the sky that makes its own light	**estrella** objeto en el cielo que produce su propia luz
	**stem** a plant part that holds up the plant	**tallo** parte de la planta que la mantiene en pie
	**structure** a part of something	**estructura** orden o distribución de las partes de algo
	**survive** to stay alive	**sobrevivir** mantenerse con vida

T

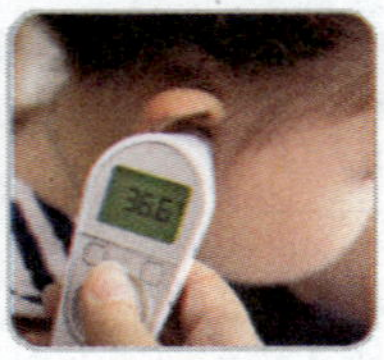	**temperature** how hot or cold something is	**temperatura** cuán caliente o frío está algo
	**texture** how something feels	**textura** cómo se siente algo al tocarlo

Español

trait a characteristic of a living thing

rasgo una característica de un ser vivo

Z

zigzag a motion with sharp turns

zigzag un movimiento que forma ángulos alternativos

Index

J

L

M

N

O

P

Q

R

S